PRISCILLA SHIRER

AWAKEN

*90 Days with the
God Who Speaks*

PUBLISHING GROUP

NASHVILLE, TENNESSEE

Published by B&H Publishing Group
Nashville, Tennessee

Dewey Decimal Classification: 242.643
Subject Heading: DEVOTIONAL LITERATURE \
CHRISTIAN LIFE \ WOMEN

1 2 3 4 5 6 7 8 • 22 21 20 19 18

For Aunt Jo

Introduction

One of the gifts that comes with age is an appreciation for some of the more simple, more commonplace things that seem mundane earlier in one's life. As the years pass, the hidden treasure to be found in humble and unpretentious virtues becomes more accentuated—things like rest, silence, and the joy of an ordinary day. The attraction toward activity and achievement lessens, becoming slowly, steadily, and appropriately replaced by an interest in more internal matters.

That's why I don't think I could have penned a devotional in my early twenties. I was too busy. Both externally and internally. If I'd tried, I'd likely have missed out on some of the personal joy to be found in the process of savoring, meditating, and pondering the many verses and lessons you'll peruse in these pages. I would have been rushing to *finish* rather than being able to glean from the *journey* that has led to this finishing point. But God is gracious, allowing me to wait until this stage in my life before publishing these devotional entrées—when my children are older, my ambitions more leveled, and my interest in timeless spiritual disciplines like prayer and Scripture meditation more intensified.

The majority of what you'll encounter here are personal whispers from God's Spirit to my own soul over the last decade. I didn't initially write them with the intention of publishing them, but simply to chronicle my own personal time with the Lord, captured in store-bought spiral notebooks filled with wide-ruled paper. To be honest, I've encountered far more insightful and discerning devotional books than this one—rich and timeless compilations from generations past, volumes that have been the framework for my own spiritual formation.

And yet however humble, what I do have, I give to you.

These passages and devotional thoughts have often challenged me, at other times encouraged me, but *every time* they have transformed me in some significant way—redirecting my focus, shifting my perspective, compelling me to action, and purifying my inner motivations. But not without investing time and quiet into the process. Somewhere along the way as I've grown older, I've discovered how much treasure is available beyond the surface reading of a Bible verse. I've learned not just to scan it but to *do business with it*—to wait underneath the revealing spotlight of God's Spirit until some aspect of my frailty is exposed and brought to the tenderness of His sanctifying work.

I want this same experience for you too. Which is why I've peppered each lesson with "He Speaks to Me" invitations—additional passages to read or look up, as well as journaling pages to help support you in your own times of sacred waiting before God. I hope they encourage you in the life-altering disciplines that will make each day's devotional worth the investment of time you'll put in. Contemplate and then record what God is showing you about Himself, about *yourself*, and what He's calling you to notice and respond to in the lives of others. Don't feel pressure to use these extra little nuances every day, but don't be too busy *not* to use them either. The praying, listening, meditating, and recording part is where the internal work—the important work—takes place. It's why devotions matter.

May these passages bring an added layer of dimension, or even just some renewed direction, to your own exchange with the Savior over the next ninety days. Whether young or old, may you be encouraged and realigned toward the simple beauty of sitting with Him, hearing Him, speaking to Him, and being enlightened by His love letter to you. I'm praying you'll be beckoned away each day from the fast-paced, temporal whirlwind of lesser (though necessary) tasks and be refocused on greater things—things that aren't applauded and appreciated by most, but are eternally recognized by One . . . the One who makes life worth living. The One who wants to *Awaken* you each day to the sound of His voice.

Now to Him who is able to keep you from stumbling and to make you stand in the presence of His glory blameless with great joy, to the only God our Savior, through Jesus Christ our Lord, be glory, majesty, dominion and authority, before all time and now and forever. Amen.
JUDE 24–25

Morning

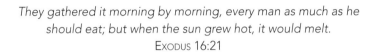

They gathered it morning by morning, every man as much as he should eat; but when the sun grew hot, it would melt.
Exodus 16:21

There's something about what happens once the sun warms up. The heat of the day's trials. The energy-stealing blaze of its pressures and events. Worries can intervene in those afternoon hours, when time is racing past so quickly, when we're certain we can't handle them within the amount of daylight that's left to us. Sometimes such stresses can be overwhelming and brazen enough to melt us in our tracks, causing the strength and resolve of our hearts to weaken and disappear.

And while this reality is as current and relevant as the day you're living right now, it's also as old as an entire generation of Old Testament Israelites. They emerged from their tents at first light each morning, eager to gather God's gift of manna that He had strewn across the ground overnight. This was a critical part of their day. An appointed activity. For they knew, once the sun ascended toward its towering position in the sky, this bread from heaven would melt away. Yes, the collection in their bowl would be more than ample for the day's requirements. They would be able to serve their families and be assured of God's provision, based on the abundant measure of what He'd given them. But they would need to wait until next morning before they'd find it new again, ready for another day's work.

Perhaps this ancient illustration depicts for us the reason why our hearts so often stir for a fresh word from God—fresh bread—early in the morning, before the heat of the day has set in.

I realize not everyone is a morning person. I realize, too, depending on your stage of life and your weekly schedule, your "morning" may occur at various, uncustomary hours of the day. But I'm convinced that *morning* is a principle, not merely a time of day. It signifies a position of priority, a place of preeminence.

Perhaps you tend to devote your first sparks of attention each day to the newscast or your email, to the various trends and updates you missed while you were sleeping. But those moments are always more valuably invested in waiting before God, feeding on His Word, listening to what He whispers to your spirit . . . while your heart is most open and refreshed and able to assimilate truth.

> Morning signifies a position of priority, a place of preeminence.

So as you move ahead into each new devotional journey, continue giving Him your first waking thought, turned upward like a breakfast bowl, ready to receive the manna He is always so faithful to supply. A fresh word and fresh mercies. Remember the "morning" principle, and prioritize the gathering of manna He offers you. Start each day and each decision with an immediate declaration of complete dependence on Him.

Because the sun's coming up soon.

Your manna is on the way.

The Lord's lovingkindnesses indeed never cease,
for His compassions never fail. They are new
every morning; great is Your faithfulness.
Lamentations 3:22–23

— He Speaks to Me —

How might this "morning" principle apply in your life right now? What can you do to be sure you're keeping God a first-place priority in every day you live and in every decision you make?

Give us each day our daily bread.
LUKE 11:3

*In the morning, O LORD, You will hear my voice; in the morning
I will order my prayer to You and eagerly watch.*
PSALM 5:3

What Do You Have?

Elisha asked her, "What can I do for you?
Tell me, what do you have in the house?"
2 KINGS 4:2 CSB

A common link nearly always exists between our needs and God's answers—a thread woven into the fabric of our relationship with the Father that, if overlooked, can cost us the most intimate and majestic experience with Him possible on this side of eternity. And in 2 Kings 4, this critical strand is clearly marked for all of us to see.

A woman, bereft of husband and financial stability, came to the prophet Elisha requesting help. Creditors were demanding payment for the debts she owed, threatening even to take her children away as part of the bargain. She was desperate. Crying out. Unable to pay.

Unable to do much at all.

The man of God graciously listened to her plight. He asked how she thought he could assist her. But before even waiting for her response to that question, he posed another, more vital one: "What do you have?" he asked. "In the house?" *What resources are already available to you?*

How easily we point to our lack. How specifically we highlight our deficiency. How quickly we become consumed with the glaring evidence of all that's working against us, the hardships that are pressing us into such desperate straits. We are far less inclined to accentuate the gifts and blessings that remain.

But Elisha, in refocusing the widow's attention on the meager pot of oil sitting there amid all her difficulty and hardship, forever changed the way she would look at her most heart-wrenching need. It can change the way we look at ours too. Like a glint of sunshine passing through ominous clouds on a dreary day, hope pierced through the darkness in her home. The foundation for a miracle was right under her nose . . . if only she would take the time and energy required to go and look. If only she would become as invested in expecting God's answers as she'd been invested in lodging her complaints.

"What do you have in the house?" In *your* house? Within *your* reach? Sometimes we wait impatiently on God when He is patiently waiting on us, waiting for us to recognize what He's already given as part of the answer to our problem. What little pot of oil have you neglected to notice? What little shred of possibility have you chosen to ignore? What little patch of time have you disparaged? What little hints of blessing have you criticized as insufficient? What little, humble beginnings have you shoved to the back shelf, considering them unworthy of being the basis for God's miraculous intentions?

> Sometimes we wait impatiently on God when He is patiently waiting on us.

Maybe the answer you've been praying for is already there—a plain-as-day response from God to your plea, immediately ready to be applied to this situation.

God will always be faithful to help you through the desperate challenges you face. Some things, obviously, only He can do. But take a good look around to see what's already at your disposal. That little jar of oil may well be the beginnings of the most spectacular move of God you've ever seen.

Seek first His kingdom and His righteousness,
and all these things will be added to you.
Matthew 6:33

— He Speaks to Me —

What are some of the "jars of oil" you might be overlooking right now that He's already provided? Make a list and keep it handy for future gratitude and reflection.

His divine power has given us everything
required for life and godliness through the knowledge
of him who called us by his own glory and goodness.
2 PETER 1:3 CSB

Honor the LORD with your possessions and with the first produce of your entire harvest; then your barns will be completely filled, and your vats will overflow with new wine.

PROVERBS 3:9–10 CSB

Come and Rest

✤

He said to them, "Come away by yourselves
to a secluded place and rest a while."
MARK 6:31

Rest is becoming a lost art in our modern culture. We've exchanged its old-fashioned value for a hectic, fast-paced, breakneck speed of life, which has slowly disintegrated our fervor and passion while simultaneously elevating our blood pressure. Packed within each twenty-four-hour time span is an unsustainable number of tasks we've placed upon ourselves, as well as demands we've allowed others to deem urgent enough to place upon us as well.

And based on our fatigue and frustration, we'd give anything to offload the burden.

But rest doesn't seem like a viable option anymore. Have we forever passed up any kind of reality that dares to include rest as part of a typical day? Or week? Or . . . month? (Or . . . *year?*)

When Jesus sent His disciples off on a specific ministry assignment in Mark 6:7–11, He didn't shield them from the fact that their journey would not be particularly easy. People would refuse to listen to them, much less give them hospitality. Any cause for excitement would be counterbalanced by any number of legitimate reasons for quitting and discouragement. They would be empowered to preach, heal, and spread the news of the kingdom, yes, but would also be exhausted on every front— physically, emotionally, and spiritually. And even after finally coming back home from their tiring journey, people would still be "coming and going," enough that the disciples "did not even have time to eat" (v. 31).

So as their first order of business upon returning, Jesus greeted them with clear instructions: "Come . . . rest a while."

It wasn't a request. It wasn't a friendly suggestion. It was Jesus' command. *Here's what you're going to do, guys.* They'd been through a lot. And much more remained to be done. But for now . . . rest . . . come and rest. At least for a little while.

Do you ever feel guilty for taking time away to regroup and recharge? Are you saddled with a sense of wasted opportunity if every space on your calendar is not filled? Are you afraid your world would stop turning if you disengaged for even a few moments? Are you concerned about losing your competitive advantage if you're not converting every moment into maximum achievement and efficiency?

Then hear the voice of your Savior welcoming you into a place where grace flows, where the Spirit refuels, and where mercy fixes what's been strained and stressed by the accumulation of life's pressures. This is the space where priorities and relationships that have been pushed out of alignment and are in need of repair get patched up and recalibrated.

> Quiet time is not an excuse for the lazy but a wise investment for the diligent.

Quiet time is not an excuse for the lazy but a wise investment for the diligent. It is for those who are committed to being active servants and followers of Jesus Christ instead of slaves to the tyranny of urgent busyness and activity. By prioritizing rest for ourselves and those we love, we may just rediscover the joy we thought had been lost forever.

My presence shall go with you,
and I will give you rest.
Exodus 33:14

— He Speaks to Me —

What would a time of deliberate rest look like for you today? This month? This year? Who are the people you can enlist to keep you accountable?

Come to me, all who are weary
and heavy-laden, and I will give you rest.
MATTHEW 11:28

_In vain you get up early and stay up late,
working hard to have enough food—yes,
he gives sleep to the one he loves._
PSALM 127:2 CSB

— Day 4 —

Run to Win

*If anyone competes as an athlete, he does not win
the prize unless he competes according to the rules.*
2 Timothy 2:5

A ny athlete worth her salt knows the rigorous training that goes into achieving victory. Success doesn't come by happenstance or magic. Her preparation must be methodical and systematic. Early mornings. Scheduled sacrifice. Any dreams of taking home a title are unlikely, if not impossible, without honing her craft to near perfection through painstaking commitment and diligence. She must build muscle, expand her stamina, and streamline her mechanics until performing them fluidly comes as natural to her as breathing.

No one accidentally backs in to athletic achievement at the highest level. *Nobody.*

Which is why it's always a shame when a well-trained athlete, having dedicated her life and limb to the pursuit, ends up throwing it away by refusing to follow the regulations of her sport. How sad to see all that practice go to waste, all that potential underutilized, all that sweat and effort amount to nothing except disqualification and disgrace because of ethical or chemical or operational shortcuts to success.

"Run in such a way that you may win" (1 Cor. 9:24). Read it again and see: the winning is not just in the running. It's in the *way* the race is run.

As believers, of course, our right standing before God has not been earned through our own spiritual exertion. The grace we've received is nothing other than "the gift of God, not a result of works" (Eph. 2:8–9 esv). *Hallelujah!* Through Christ's sacrifice alone we have "been released from the Law" (Rom. 7:6) and from its binding effects on us for our salvation. And yet the Bible clearly marks the pathway that leads to a thriving life of Christian victory and blessing. It's really not much of a secret. God has made known the lines of demarcation within which you can experience success in all the events you've entered in life—as a parent, a wife, a friend, a leader—all the places where you're determined to excel in serving Him.

Don't forfeit the opportunity through rebellion or illegitimate shortcuts or spiritual indolence. Don't throw away the things you've been called, equipped, and prepared to become by refusing to run within the divine boundaries of obedience the Lord has set up for your benefit. Run the race not only with endurance and diligence, but also with careful, watchful submission to His Word. When you're tempted to put yourself in a better position by bending a biblical principle, stay anchored to the right path. When the Spirit alerts you to a ground rule (which feels in the moment to be unnecessary and inconvenient), don't recoil in rebellion. Deny yourself and follow Him. Run to win. Trust your Father to keep you on the winning trajectory, the one that leads to hearing "well done" and enjoying the long-lasting satisfaction of eternal accomplishments—the only achievements that really matter anyway.

> The Bible clearly marks the pathway that leads to a thriving life of Christian victory and blessing.

Continue in the things you have learned and become convinced of, knowing from whom you have learned them.
2 TIMOTHY 3:14

— He Speaks to Me —

What are some basic, biblical guidelines you've gotten away from prioritizing? Ask the Lord to bring them to mind.

Be doers of the word and not hearers only, deceiving yourselves.
JAMES 1:22 CSB

In all your ways acknowledge Him,
and He will make your paths straight.
PROVERBS 3:6

Wait for It

〰

There was a man in Jerusalem, whose name was Simeon, and this man was righteous and devout, waiting for the consolation of Israel, and the Holy Spirit was upon him.
LUKE 2:25 ESV

A shooting star. I'm almost certain that's what it was.

I casually glanced upward into the evening sky while walking groceries into the house from the car, and there it was—the tail end of a shooting star jetting through the heavens. Or *was* it? I couldn't tell for sure. It all happened so fast. You know how it is—one of those moments when you wish you could somehow rewind the tape, go back a minute and a half ago, call the kids outside to come watch with you, and then be standing there, head upturned, eyes peeled upon the spot. If you knew it was coming, if you knew what to be watching for, you could catch the whole thing from beginning to end.

God is moving and working all around us. But more often than not, we've got our head down, fixed on getting through the day. We're not thinking beyond the immediate present, not looking for indications of God's activity, just looking at our watch and our list of things to do, wondering how we'll ever be able to get it all done.

Simeon, however, was a man who was "waiting" on the Messiah. He had his day job, I'm sure, things that needed to be routinely maintained and accomplished. But he was simultaneously on the alert, always looking for something—Someone special and life-changing. The Holy Spirit told him the Deliverer was near. And because he wanted nothing more than to see this promised One with his own eyes, he postured his heart in a continual state of holy anticipation—just in case this could be the day when the Son of God showed up on the landscape of his life, changing everything for him and for everyone else around him.

That's why when Mary and Joseph entered the temple grounds, Simeon saw much, much more than everyone else, who likely saw nothing more than an ordinary Jewish family. He recognized instead the face of humankind's salvation—"a light of revelation to the Gentiles, and the glory of Your people Israel" (Luke 2:32).

Is your heart fixed today to recognize the presence of God? To see His fingerprints and hear His voice? The events that others call coincidence, will you recognize them as sovereign providence? Ask the Lord to sharpen your spiritual senses so that you catch a glimpse of His glory. Focus your expectation. Lean forward or on tiptoe. Resist the inclination to be so caught up in the temporal that you miss seeing the eternal. Scan the horizon for where His voice is calling out to you or where His fingerprints are working on your behalf. Be alert. Be present. Be fully engaged in the day stretched out before you.

> Is your heart fixed today to recognize the presence of God?

He'll be there. Waiting to be seen by anyone watching and waiting.

My soul waits for the Lord more than the watchmen for the morning; indeed, more than the watchmen for the morning.
PSALM 130:6

— He Speaks to Me —

Watch for Him today. Diligently ask Him to show you where He is working, where His Spirit is actively moving. Then come back here and write about it.

_Joshua said to the people, "Consecrate yourselves,
for tomorrow the L<small>ORD</small> will do wonders among you."_
J<small>OSHUA</small> 3:5

As for me, I will watch expectantly for the LORD;
I will wait for the God of my salvation. My God will hear me.
MICAH 7:7

Looking and Seeing

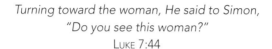

*Turning toward the woman, He said to Simon,
"Do you see this woman?"*
LUKE 7:44

L ooking and seeing are two different things. They represent the same gap in attention that exists between hearing and listening. One is merely the physical, almost involuntary action of a functioning human body, while the other action requires the willing cooperation of the heart. Many a rebellious teenager has acceded to the former (looking, not seeing—hearing, not listening) while showing little interest or regard for the latter. In fact, many a rebellious grownup has done it too, if we're being quite honest about it.

This duplicitous posture is the stock-in-trade of the busy, the self-consumed, and the haughtily superior. Whenever we're certain that our own schedules and reputations are the most important to maintain, we lack the sensitivity and compassion needed to pay attention to what someone else is saying and truly digest what they're communicating. We fail to see—to really see—what's happening in someone else's heart, and thus we fail to offer sympathy, compassion, and resolution.

In this biblical moment from Luke 7, Simon the Pharisee had just witnessed the shocking spectacle of a lewd woman sneaking uninvited into his home during a dinner party, and pouring her worshipful tears and perfume on the feet of Jesus. Every eye in the room had looked on, including Simon's—horrified, taken aback. They all saw her, but Jesus specifically asked Simon to *look again.*

Because if he could really see her, he would know that this woman—this unsavory looking woman—had come seeking forgiveness from her Savior. She had come seeking forgiveness for sins no worse or more heinous than those committed by the smug and self-righteous. And if he had *seen* this in her, rather than merely gawking at her, his hypocrisy would have melted into humility. His critique would have morphed into compassion. His inclination for judging would have turned the camera of inspection toward himself, so that he could have walked out of that place with the same gifts she did—saving faith and blessed "peace" from Jesus Himself (Luke 7:50).

How different would your own relationships and encounters with others be if you, by God's Spirit, could heighten your *looking* into *seeing*? How much more fruitful could your personal impact become on an everyday basis if you elevated your *hearing* into *listening*?

> As you walk into this coming day, don't just look. See.

You would become a choice instrument in the hand of God, prepared for His purposes, propelled by His passion, moved to displays of grace and mercy toward the hurting victims of a lost and dying world.

As you walk into this coming day, don't just look. *See.* Ask the Lord to give you eyes of discernment to detect layers below the surface, and to respond in a way that will honor Him and bless others.

Elisha prayed, "LORD, please open his eyes and let him see."
2 KINGS 6:17 CSB

— He Speaks to Me —

Think back on some of the things that have occurred in your life, simply within the past twenty-four hours. What are some of the things you missed the opportunity to really *see*?

Lord, when did we see You hungry, or thirsty, or a stranger, or naked, or sick, or in prison, and did not take care of You?
Matthew 25:44

The hearing ear and the seeing eye,
the LORD has made both of them.
PROVERBS 20:12

Give and Receive

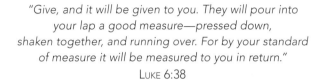

*"Give, and it will be given to you. They will pour into
your lap a good measure—pressed down,
shaken together, and running over. For by your standard
of measure it will be measured to you in return."*
Luke 6:38

Ever since I was a little girl, our family's summers have always included a week of church camp. Still today with my husband and three boys, we load up the car and drive two hours into the wilds of east Texas for seven full days of water sports, late-night ice cream sundaes, and early morning trail rides on horseback. On the last day, we head out into the woods, sauntering to the easy gait of horse's hooves, before dismounting at a cabin that's already awake with the luscious aromas of country breakfast and hot coffee.

But before we go inside, there's one place we always go first. Perched beside the wraparound porch is an old-fashioned pump where we can wash our hands from the dusty, grimy effects of our morning trail ride. It's the kind of vintage pump where you crank its metal handle up and down to get it started. But before any cool refreshment can start flowing *out*, we must first pour a quick stream of water *in*. A small container that hangs nearby provides enough to prime the pump. With just this tiny amount of water, the well from which it draws its deep supply starts to gush with more than enough water to wash our hands, splash our face, pat our sweaty necks and arms, rinse off our dirty feet. The water we invest comes back not in the same measure we gave it, but in more bountiful amounts than we even have the capacity to receive.

Such is life in the kingdom of God. Not only is His nature one of lavish, unbridled generosity, but He often responds to the specific essence of our giving. "Do not judge," Jesus said, "and you will not be judged. Do not condemn, and you will not be condemned. Forgive, and you will be forgiven" (Luke 6:37 CSB). Not that we do our giving for the purpose of receiving. After all, the extravagant gift of His grace is more than reason enough for our undying gratitude and sacrifice. But when we give grace to others, we experience God's grace in even greater abundance. When we give kindness and mercy and unconditional love, His own love exceeds our investment and rejuvenates our soul.

When we forgive others of the things they've said or done, we're able to relish in the full breadth of His forgiveness, covering sins we once doubted could ever be dealt with, much less washed away.

> God does not give to us in scanty, meager proportions.

Our God does not give to us in scanty, meager proportions, but in overflows, abundances, and excesses. He gives back much more than our meager outlay would merit, but He does it so that there's enough left over to spare—enough to prime the pump for the next go-around.

So give. Even in your deficient places. *Especially in those places.* Give, even when what you're giving is more than you feel like you can afford. Remember, your God intends to return it all to you, "pressed down, shaken together, and running over."

Little children, let us not love in word
or speech, but in action and in truth.
1 JOHN 3:18 CSB

— He Speaks to Me —

What is an area of your life where you feel a sense of lack and deficiency right now (time, finances, patience, passions, hope)? How can you give to another person in that area today? Make a plan, and then see what happens when you do.

time - patience - Hope

*A generous person will be enriched, and the one
who gives a drink of water will receive water.*
PROVERBS 11:25 CSB

God is able to make all grace abound to you,
so that always having all sufficiency in everything,
you may have an abundance for every good deed.
2 Corinthians 9:8

No More Circles

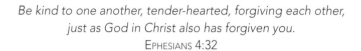

Be kind to one another, tender-hearted, forgiving each other,
just as God in Christ also has forgiven you.
EPHESIANS 4:32

The pony had once been part of a circus act, relegated to walking in circles, day after day, year after year, doing whatever his handlers required of him. But after being retired from the traveling show, his new home became a lush, spacious pasture out in the country, abounding in opportunity for exploration and discovery. Yet even in this newfound place of freedom, he couldn't seem to escape his old pattern of life. He still continued walking mostly in circles, round and round, day in and day out—apparently not knowing any other way to operate.

These circles represent the burden of unforgiveness—how it defines us, restrains us, controls us, until over time it becomes our legacy, our pattern of living, the first thing others notice about us. Though surrounded on all sides by the new spaces that each season of life brings, unforgiveness forces us to stay rutted, one-dimensional, thinly sliced, unable to experience the joys and freedoms that exist beyond the periphery of our closely guarded pain. It fits us with blinders, keeping us relegated to memories of the offenses done against us, to the artificial boundaries created by yesterday's disappointments—a circle of mundane, cheerless living that's far beneath the abundant life we've been created to enjoy.

Always those circles. Nothing but circles. Please, God, no more circles.

I realize it's hard to forgive. Sometimes painfully hard. Perhaps, though, you've seen the pointlessness of it, the regressive nature of it, and you've *tried* to forgive. You've genuinely *thought* you were there. You felt like you were branching out beyond where the memories had held you for so long. But then here it came again—another betrayal, another broken promise, another blow to your fragile trust. And as a result, deeper hurt. Closed loops. Tighter circles.

> Unforgiveness keeps us relegated to the artificial boundaries created by yesterday's disappointments.

But God wants you released from the self-imposed bondage. His Word exhorts each of us to tear up the ongoing record of others' wrongdoing, same as He did with us when He "erased the certificate of debt, with its obligations, that was against us and opposed to us . . . nailing it to the cross" (Col. 2:14 CSB). He now invites you to unload all the responsibility you may feel for enforcing justice on others, leaving "room for the wrath of God" (Rom. 12:19), leaving the job to One who can more wisely deal with it.

Forgiveness is certainly a miracle—a supernatural outworking of God's Spirit within you, enabling you to extend something to the people in your life that you could never do otherwise. But when, by His help, you choose to forgive, He will remove you from your old ruts of walking space, setting you free to breathe the fresh air of His goodness. He will change the geometry of your life from endless circles into the best shape your heart has ever been before.

Forgive us our debts, as we also have forgiven our debtors.
MATTHEW 6:12

— He Speaks to Me —

While unforgiveness feels safe, feels necessary, feels protective of your heart, what valuable things has it cost you? What does it hold you back from experiencing? From being?

If anyone is in Christ, he is a new creature;
the old things passed away; behold, new things have come.
2 CORINTHIANS 5:17

I, even I, am the one who wipes out your transgressions
for My own sake, and I will not remember your sins.
Isaiah 43:25

Finishing Well

---✦---

> *"And now it has pleased You to bless the house of*
> *Your servant, that it may continue forever before You;*
> *for You, O LORD, have blessed, and it is blessed forever."*
> 1 CHRONICLES 17:27

Could anyone other than David have been a more natural choice to oversee the construction of Israel's first permanent house of worship? Imagine the disappointment, perhaps even the confusion he must have felt when trying to digest the news he'd been given by the prophet Nathan that someone else would enjoy this honor instead?

David was faced with a choice: either selfishly insist on fulfilling his own ambitions, or step aside and willingly pass on the baton to the one whom God had appointed to complete the task. He chose wisely. Instead of succumbing to hubris or acceding to selfish ambition, he cleared the way for the next one in line. He didn't scramble to maintain his position or usurp the assignment God had delegated to another. He trusted. He submitted. He finished well . . . by *not finishing.*

I wonder how many divine missions, mandates, and ministries are aborted by self-minded Christians who refuse to relinquish control of the task to those who follow in their footsteps. I wonder how many worthy pursuits have lost their spiritual relevance and vitality because someone greedily clung to their personal ownership of it, rather than cheerfully stepping aside, encouraging its growth and maturity into a new generation.

One of the more difficult nuances of victorious Christian living is that of staying sensitive to the Spirit's timing, of knowing when He's whispering, "Enough now, My child." Only the truly humble heart will comply when it's time to let others carry the reins of responsibility forward while their own assignment shifts to another role. But just as an Olympic relay is dependent on each successful exchange of the baton, so are churches, ministries, families, and visions dependent on faithful leaders who will yield power when it's someone else's turn to carry the torch.

"Finishing well" can sometimes mean not seeing the full end of what you started, but rather stepping away so others can share in the victory of a race well run.

The fact is, the glorious building that rose from the city of David is still remembered, all these centuries later, as "Solomon's Temple." Before its demoralizing destruction at the hand of pagan invaders centuries later, its opulence was known far and wide as being reminiscent of its builder's esteem. *Solomon's Temple.* And yet Solomon's success was largely due to David's selfless release, and also to something more—something beautiful and staggering in its generosity. According to 1 Chronicles 22, David used the remainder of his lifetime to collect the materials, delegate the workforce, fund the expenses, and enthusiastically validate his son before the entire nation. He paved the path for his replacement's success.

> He trusted. He submitted. He finished well . . . by *not finishing.*

Not everything is yours to finish. Many tasks of great kingdom importance may not be wholly synchronized with your own lifetime or your particular generation. Still, choose to gratefully be a part of what God is doing by fully investing yourself in His greater work.

Yes, the work is *His.* And since it is, release it back to Him whenever He asks you to, trusting that the scope of it will be beyond your wildest imagination.

Let us run with endurance the race that is set before us,
fixing our eyes on Jesus, the author and perfecter of faith.
Hebrews 12:1–2

— He Speaks to Me —

Is there a project or ambition you're clinging to, out of fear of being replaced or being unknown? If so, what is it? Entrust it to the Lord, and ask Him to give you the courage to loosen your grip.

He who plants and he who waters are one; but each will receive his own reward according to his own labor.
1 CORINTHIANS 3:8

*I have fought the good fight, I have finished
the course, I have kept the faith.*
2 TIMOTHY 4:7

The Difference

---
*

*"But since my servant Caleb has a different spirit
and has remained loyal to me, I will bring him into the land
where he has gone, and his descendants will inherit it."*
NUMBERS 14:24 CSB

The Lord had freed ancient Israel from four centuries of bondage in Egypt, opening up for them what had once been an unthinkable opportunity to inherit "a land flowing with milk and honey" (Exod. 3:8). But at a key moment in their pilgrimage to Canaan, a majority of Israel's population shrank back from the daring endeavor of claiming God's promise. They chose the safer route, the more easily explainable route, the more reasonable and protective route, rather than the guaranteed, take-no-prisoners route that led to conquering a whole new realm of territory for themselves and their children.

That's why only two of the original two million travelers— Joshua and Caleb—ended up walking as victorious landowners on Canaan's soil. Factor it down, and you have a profound spiritual equation.

Individually, these men were *one in a million.*

And what set them apart, the Scripture says (of Caleb, but surely of Joshua too), is that they possessed "a different spirit." They didn't need to fit in. They didn't need to be liked. They didn't base their conclusions on the majority report. They didn't depend on the approval of their friends for determining which path they would choose to walk. They simply hit the dirt road toward the Promised Land and never looked back. They believed that the same God who could bring a mighty Pharaoh to his knees could do the same to any other enemy who stood in the way of His plans being fulfilled for His people. As a result, these two—and *only* these two—who'd begun their lives as slaves in Egypt were able to complete them as free men in God's country.

Because . . . *they were different.*

Abundant living mandates different living—different even from other believers who may be complacent with their freedom, lulled to sleep in their wilderness wanderings. To experience everything God intends, a difference is required. One in which your thought processes, self-disciplines, and most pressing choices carve out a narrow road that is not often tread. One on which you will nearly always walk alone. Alien. Stranger. Sore Thumb.

Are you willing? To be the one in a million?

> Abundant living mandates different living.

The traveling conditions are rarely smooth sailing when heading in the direction of abundant living. The places where God's presence and provision—His milk and honey—abound are where bold belief in His promises take priority over man's acceptance and affirmation. Ask the Father—the Deliverer—to give you the kind of courage by His Spirit that would make you willing to stand out from the crowd when called for.

The difference will be worth it.

The gate is small and the way is narrow
that leads to life, and there are few who find it.
MATTHEW 7:14

— He Speaks to Me —

How are you feeling compelled right now to be different? How is God making this clear?

_____

_____

_____

_____

_____

_____

_____

_____

_____

_____

_____

_____

_____

The fear of man brings a snare, but he who
trusts in the Lord will be exalted.
Proverbs 29:25

Peter and the apostles answered,
"We must obey God rather than men."
ACTS 5:29

Seen in a Different Light

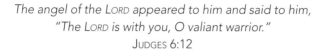

*The angel of the L<small>ORD</small> appeared to him and said to him,
"The L<small>ORD</small> is with you, O valiant warrior."*
J<small>UDGES</small> 6:12

For several evenings while getting ready for bed, I'd noticed in the mirror an angry, dark bruise on my lower back. Where had it come from? Should I be worried? Why wasn't it getting any better? And why, when I finally asked my husband to look at it, did he dismissively say he didn't see anything?

"What? It's right here," I said, pointing to the ugly splotch I could clearly see reflected in my closet mirror. Coming closer, he scanned my back for the same blemish I was seeing. Nope, nothing, until—"Oh," he finally said, apparently locating it, but without the same sense of concern in his voice I was expecting to hear. Instead, he sort of laughed while taking both my arms in his two brawny hands, scooting me about six inches to the right. "Gone now?"

I looked back in the mirror. Astonished that my husband had performed a modern-day miracle. He was right. It was gone. The dark patch I'd mistaken as a problem area on my body had been nothing more than a shadow in the room. A simple shift, a mere change in perspective changed everything.

The Old Testament shadow that had long been cast across Gideon's life had caused him to see himself as timid, fearful, doubtful, incapable. Like others of his countrymen, his entire existence had been discolored by the silhouette of their dreaded enemies (the Midianites), leaving him a defeated shell of a man, intimidated into hiding, not wanting to attract notice or draw attention to himself. But when the angel of the Lord appeared one day, while Gideon was threshing wheat in a shaded winepress to keep from being seen, the surprising words of an angel tugged him out of the shadows and into the clarifying light of Yahweh's perspective.

"The LORD is with you, O valiant warrior."

He was "valiant." *And* he was a "warrior." Despite the shadows, God considered him capable of brave exploits and sent the pre-incarnate Christ to tell him so. Thus began a series of changes that transformed Gideon from an insecure coward into a gallant captain of Israel's fighting men. By revealing an inner potential that no one (neither Gideon or anybody else) had ever noticed, the angel moved him into position for God to bring out a courage He could use to inspire a nation to victory.

A simple shift, a mere change in perspective changed everything.

Take a good look at yourself and the reality of your current circumstances. Has the shadow of your situation cast a gloomy haze on how you see yourself? Do you doubt what God's Word says about you, based on what you see when you look in the mirror—that you are loved, forgiven, known, and thoroughly provided for?

God's Spirit is tugging you out of those shadows today, clearing away the stains you've misread as permanent fixtures on your soul. May the One who redeemed you by His own blood redefine your identity in the light of His mercy, promise, and power.

You are a chosen race, a royal priesthood, a holy nation,
a people for God's own possession, so that you may
proclaim the excellencies of Him who has called you
out of darkness into His marvelous light.
1 PETER 2:9

— He Speaks to Me —

Record some of the differences between how the Scripture defines you and how you define yourself.

See what kind of love the Father has given to us,
that we should be called children of God; and so we are.
1 JOHN 3:1 ESV

What then shall we say to these things?
If God is for us, who is against us?
Romans 8:31

Functional Leprosy

❧

Naaman, captain of the army of the king of Aram,
was a great man with his master, and highly respected,
because by him the LORD had given victory to Aram.
The man was also a valiant warrior, but he was a leper.
2 KINGS 5:1

Social media has made voyeurs of us all. We carefully study and judge the lives of others, discovering things about them by stealth that we might never ask in person. But what we've mainly gathered from all our snooping is the pressure for keeping up airs. So when creating our own social media personas, we cleverly conceal the reality of our private struggles, opting instead for an exaggerated, plastic version of the truth. We mask our hurts and weakness and deficiencies, promoting a caricature that may technically resemble ourselves under carefully calculated lighting, yet is vigilant to hide the flaws underneath.

But perhaps modern technologies are not entirely to blame for these attempts to put a better face forward. A bit of writing that dates back to the fifth chapter of 2 Kings, for example, opens with a long list of accomplishments concerning Naaman. His high-level bio sketch contains elements of accolade, appreciation, achievement, and admiration. He was a celebrated leader in the Syrian army. He'd accrued the respect of his subordinates and earned favor with his king. "A great man . . . a valiant warrior," all the things you'd want included in your viewable profile. And yet peeking out from underneath the veneer of his success was this one little mention of something that couldn't stay hidden any longer.

Naaman was . . . a leper.

As a career fighting man of brave and noble reputation, the last thing he wanted anyone to know was that he suffered from this worst kind of ailment, one that found little compassion from others and certainly no possibility of cure. Leprosy was the kind of disease that could lie dormant for more than a decade before revealing itself in an obvious, public way. Until then, the sick person could strategically cover proof of its existence with careful clothing choices and self-protective mannerisms. In this way, it was possible to live as a *functional leper.*

We've now mastered the art of functional leprosy—sick and blemished and hurting on the inside, but all polished and buttoned-up on the outside. Perhaps anger boils in our heart. Perhaps a passionless, stale marriage barely exists within our home. Perhaps anxiety eats away at our peace of mind. Perhaps addiction robs us of freedom. Perhaps unforgiveness numbs our soul. Perhaps a lapse in integrity cloaks us with guilt. Yet we conceal these private pains from public knowledge with perfectly composed selfies. We're dying in plain sight. For surely, this hidden leprosy will be the death of us.

Unless we let authenticity heal us first.

If we will lay ourselves bare before the Lord and be honest about ourselves with trustworthy sojourners in the body of Christ, we can be restored from what's killing us. Today is the day for openness and vulnerability, entrusting our real selves to the loving eyes of the Father.

> We've mastered the art of functional leprosy.

Confess your sins to one another, and pray for one another so that you may be healed.
JAMES 5:16

— He Speaks to Me —

Pray with David today, "Search me, O God, and know my heart" (Ps. 139:23). Then by His Spirit, be brave enough to deal with the things He brings to light.

He who conceals his transgressions will not prosper, but he who confesses and forsakes them will find compassion.
PROVERBS 28:13

*Most gladly, therefore, I will rather boast about
my weaknesses, so that the power of Christ may dwell in me.*
2 CORINTHIANS 12:9

Where Would Jesus Be?

⚜

He said to them, "Why is it that you were looking for Me?
Did you not know that I had to be in My Father's house?"
LUKE 2:49

It's the only patch of Scripture that really gives us any window into Jesus' life as a child. And strikingly, it's a mother's worst nightmare. *Her son was missing.*

Following their attendance at the Passover festival, Mary figured Jesus was probably in safe company with others in the caravan headed back home. Instead, He was nowhere to be found. Imagine the maddening thoughts that went through her mind, convincing her with each step that the worst must have happened. Picture how desperate she was to see that face again, to run and embrace her missing son, to hold on to what she thought she'd lost.

Twenty-four hours soon turned to forty-eight, which ballooned to seventy-two. It had been almost a hundred now—four days since she'd seen Him—a full day walking away from Him unknowingly, and three days looking high and low, backward and forward, calling out for Him and asking people if they'd seen Him. And yet she still didn't know where He was, or where else to look for Him.

But then, finally, she caught a glimpse of Him among a knot of religious teachers in the temple, "listening to them and asking them questions. And all who heard Him were amazed at His understanding and His answers" (Luke 2:46–47).

Mary was amazed as well. Astonished. And relieved, I'm sure. This child she thought she'd lost through her negligence was back within reach, a sight for a panicked mother's eyes.

There He was—engaged in the fundamental calling that she (more than anyone else) knew He was here to perform. "Did you not know," He'd asked her, "that I had to be in My Father's house?" (v. 49). No, but . . . yes. Somehow she did. Or should have. Why hadn't she searched there sooner?

And maybe I'd ask the same thing to you today, if you've not seemed able to find Jesus lately amid the ongoing rhythms of your life, to feel His presence with you, to sense His voice, His power, His guidance, His direction, His peace. No need to look high and low, in out-of-the-way places, in unusual circumstances or New Age ideologies. He's always there in the places and spaces where He has eternally promised to meet with us—in prayer, in His Word, in your heart. Every time you bend your humbled knees before Him, He is there. Every time you soak in His love letter to you, He is there. Every time your soul dances to the lilt of His Spirit within, there He is.

> He's always there in the places and spaces where He has eternally promised to meet with His children.

Closer than you think. Right where He told you He'd be.

You will call upon Me and come and pray to Me,
and I will listen to you. You will seek Me and find Me
when you search for Me with all your heart.
JEREMIAH 29:12–13

— He Speaks to Me —

Renew your commitment to the fundamental disciplines of your faith—prayer, meditation on Scripture, worship. You will always find Him here.

Let us draw near with confidence to the throne of grace, so that we may receive mercy and find grace to help in time of need.
HEBREWS 4:16

Whoever confesses that Jesus is the Son of God,
God abides in him, and he in God.
1 JOHN 4:15

One Good Reason

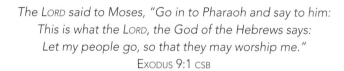

*The LORD said to Moses, "Go in to Pharaoh and say to him:
This is what the LORD, the God of the Hebrews says:
Let my people go, so that they may worship me."*
EXODUS 9:1 CSB

I'm a simple girl. I like things simple. That's why the simplicity of Yahweh's objective when freeing His people from slavery intrigues me.

God's reason for wanting His children OUT of Egypt, OUT of bondage, OUT of slavery, OUT from under a cruel taskmaster, was NOT primarily to take them into the Promised Land. It was NOT primarily to shower great blessings upon them. It was NOT primarily to show them His remarkable power. All of those things would be theirs, of course, if they followed Him away from their forefathers' long centuries of bondage in Egypt, if they followed Him on to their destiny as a people. They would see incredible things; they would witness miraculous provision; they would be part of repeated deliverances that continually offered them freedom from their greatest fears and hungers.

But God's real reason, His primary reason, for delivering them from the hand of Pharaoh was much simpler and more revealing of His heart. *He freed them so they could be unencumbered in their worship of Him.* Undistracted intimacy. Undivided attention. Wholly focused on their Deliverer . . . in worship.

At least a dozen times throughout the deliverance process, He expressed this simple aim: "Let my people go, so that they may worship me." It's what He'd been saying before Moses' return trip to Egypt even began in Exodus 4, and it's what He continued to say throughout all those many appeals for Israel's freedom before the stubborn defiance of Pharaoh. "I will take you for My people, and I will be your God; and you shall know that I am the LORD your God, who brought you out from under the burdens of the Egyptians" (Exod. 6:7). "You shall not worship any other god, for the LORD, whose name is Jealous, is a jealous God" (Exod. 34:14). He was—and is—possessive of His people and passionate about His relationship with them.

From the beginning of time, He desired connection with His children. It started in Eden when He walked with Adam and Eve, and it continued into the New Testament when He clothed Himself with humanity to walk among humankind. It continues still today as He woos us to Himself through the Holy Spirit. And it's why He wants us released from the power of sin—so that because of His grace poured out upon us, we "might bring praise to his glory" (Eph. 1:12 CSB). He wants us to be free and unencumbered in worship. Unshackled. Showering Him in worship, a worship He inspires in our hearts. It's what He wanted from His children way back then, and it's still what He wants today.

> He was—and is—passionate about His relationship with His people.

May His focus remain our focus. May we refuse to elevate any other intentions—no matter how virtuous—above the one main thing for which He set us free.

To worship.

An hour is coming, and now is, when the true
worshipers will worship the Father in spirit and truth;
for such people the Father seeks to be His worshipers.
JOHN 4:23

— He Speaks to Me —

How can you shower Him in praise today? Write out a litany of worship to Him. Be specific. Be grateful.

Let not the oppressed return dishonored;
let the afflicted and needy praise Your name.
Psalm 74:21

*So that we who had already put our hope
in Christ might bring praise to his glory.*
EPHESIANS 1:12 CSB

Ego Monster

A man's pride will bring him low,
but a humble spirit will obtain honor.
PROVERBS 29:23

Apart of us—in all of us—longs for a nod of approval from someone. And the more someones we can get it from, the better. From the supervisor who says we're doing an exceptionally good job this quarter. From the ministry director at church who thanks us for serving so well and showing such talent. From the toothy grin of our little one, throwing his arms around us and saying, "I love you."

Yet underneath much of this generic desire for approval lies the scariest of all monsters. And if we aren't aware of its strength and strategy, it can eat us alive.

In a dark, hidden room deep inside us where it lurks, one of its hairy appendages is almost always too unruly to be tamed. The ego monster pokes through a tiny crevice in our soul's lockbox, creating just enough space for the whole devastating ogre to eventually emerge. Then, when we are offended at being overlooked or outperformed or underappreciated in some way, it lurches toward the surface, showing up in our furrowed brow and pasted-on grin. How dare someone else receive what we deserve? How dare we not be selected for the position when we're so much more capable and qualified?

But oddly, success is often the antagonist that stirs the monster into its most irrepressible frenzy. Applause and opportunity are its food, its fuel. They cause it to grow larger and more voracious, bigger, stronger—until layer by layer, it begins dismantling the veneer of false humility we'd been creating throughout our lives in hopes of disguising it.

That's when we start to realize what others have already suspected. That's when we discover that our noble motivations, truth be told, were mostly just self-satisfying excuses. That's when it becomes all too clear we've been duped. Ego has pulled the wool over our eyes. *Gotcha.* The monster has claimed another victim.

It is only the humility that comes from God's Spirit, not our need for impressing people and receiving affirmation, that will allow us to fulfill His calling, solely for the pleasure of obeying Him and living for His purposes. By His strength alone will we be committed to the discipline His mission requires, even if—*especially if*—it comes with little thanks, reward, or recognition at the end.

The approval of others is never a suitable replacement for the Father's.

Applause is not the grand prize waiting at the end of our life's many endeavors. The approval of others is never a suitable replacement for the Father's. So fight this monster instead of trying to hide it. Bring it out into the open where it has no other choice today but to sit by and watch us while we take all the acclaim it tells us we deserve, and place it straight at the feet of Jesus.

*It is not good to eat too much honey
or to seek glory after glory.*
PROVERBS 25:27 CSB

— He Speaks to Me —

How have you sensed pride creeping in lately? What are some proactive steps you can take to slay it?

Do nothing from selfishness or empty conceit, but with humility of mind regard one another as more important than yourselves.
PHILIPPIANS 2:3

*Not to us, O Lord, not to us, but to Your name give glory
because of Your lovingkindness, because of Your truth.*
Psalm 115:1

More than Meets the Eye

🐝

What no eye has seen, no ear has heard, and no human heart has conceived—God has prepared these things for those who love him.
1 Corinthians 2:9 csb

Your view, no matter how breathtaking and beautiful or how grim and dismal, is not the full scope of reality. Whatever is seen—all that can be measured or documented or quantified with the five physical senses or through the lens of your current emotional state—is not all that is meant to be seen. The physical cannot fully grasp the comprehensiveness of the spiritual. God's work is behind the scenes, beyond all the obvious readouts. If we limit the scope for our hopefulness to what's immediately visible, we'll get an inaccurate reading on any scenario we're seeking to evaluate. Believers must live by faith, by believing what they cannot yet see.

This has always been the case.

In 1 Kings 18, during the reign of wicked King Ahab and the oppression of a three-year drought, most Israelites scanning the western sky would think the tiny wisp of a cloud "as small as a man's hand" (v. 44) was nothing to get too excited about. It didn't even qualify as an official cloud really. More of a cloud *fragment*, a cloud *baby*, hoping it could grow up to actually be a cloud someday. Yet to ears like the prophet Elijah's, which were tuned in to heaven's frequency, this hazy puff of moisture in the heavens had "the sound of the roar of a heavy shower" (v. 41). To eyes looking for more than the average answers to average prayers, it wouldn't be long before "the sky grew black with clouds and wind" (v. 45) and God's awesome rain-making ability would be put on full, drenching display.

This is God's way—preparing unfathomable things, even when only the slightest hints of them can be barely detected. This is God's way—crafting supernatural downpours behind the tiniest, most innocuous cloud cover. We must live in light of this. It's what shifts us from doubt and worry to stability and faith. It's what enables us to trust that the Father is able to come through at the perfect moment, no matter how far removed the possibility seems from our current vantage point. It's what helps us pick up on the fact that His forecast is predicting something diametrically opposed to what the weather looks like right now.

> This is God's way—preparing unfathomable things, even when only the slightest hints of them can be barely detected.

This was Elijah's privilege. And it is ours as well.

Remember that even a little cloud of hope, when God's Word is behind it, points toward a downpour of promise, potential, and possibility. Even His silence and seeming slowness are only the quiet buildup to a thunderous revelation of His glory. So train your prayerful eyes toward the heavens. Prepare for Him to act in His own wise time and for the honor of His faithful name. Things may not seem too impressive and assuring at the moment, but the pitter-patter of His activity could change the weather conditions in your life before you know it.

Hope does not disappoint, because the love of God has been poured out within our hearts through the Holy Spirit who was given to us.
ROMANS 5:5

— He Speaks to Me —

What can you proactively do today to shift your perspective from doubt to faith, from anxiety to hopeful expectation?

_Faith is the assurance of things hoped for,
the conviction of things not seen._
HEBREWS 11:1

It is good to wait quietly for salvation from the LORD.
LAMENTATIONS 3:26 CSB

Nineveh. Now.

---

*The word of the LORD came to Jonah the son of
Amittai saying, "Arise, go to Nineveh the great city and cry
against it, for their wickedness has come up before Me."*
JONAH 1:1–2

Nineveh was a terrible town that boasted an ominous reputation for inflicting physical and psychological terror
on its enemies. Primarily on the Israelites. So God's command to Jonah, to "go to Nineveh the great city and cry against
it," was patently unthinkable. Though perhaps softened to our
ears by its common placement in children's Bible storybooks,
this divine order to an Israelite who'd experienced the terrors of
the Ninevites was nothing short of shocking. "Go to Nineveh?"
No, Lord. Anywhere but Nineveh.

What's your Nineveh? Where's the place you never want to
go? Is it to the imprisoned? Is it to atheists on the Internet? Is it
to a certain foreign country with weather too frigid to suit your
penchant for more tropical climates?

Or maybe your Nineveh is not a *place* at all. Maybe it's
a *person*—someone that God's Spirit, speaking through His
Word, is pressing you to forgive and show compassion toward—
an ex-spouse, an abusive parent, a betraying friend. Feels like
such a pointless undertaking, sure of accomplishing nothing
but putting you into an emotional tailspin. The mere thought
of being gracious and empathetic toward them is more than you
can stomach. Like Jonah, you can think of a million reasons for
hanging back or running away. And yet "the word of the LORD"
has come, not much unlike how it came to Jonah. It keeps pop-
ping up in Sunday sermons and Bible study groups, in offhand

stories you hear on Christian radio and in middle-of-the-night impressions on your heart. It's God, plain and simple. You know it beyond a reasonable doubt. His Spirit is pressing you forward in the direction of that person, place, or thing that you never thought would come calling with your name on it. Can you really say no? But can you really say yes? To Nineveh?

Yes.

Now.

This is the only answer that's certain of yielding a harvest, the only answer that's sure of being infused with God's blessing and a demonstration of His work. To say no is to invite the chaotic distress and confusion that put Jonah in the belly of a great fish. But to say yes is to embark toward an experience that has God's fingerprints written all over it, like when "Nineveh believed in God . . . from the greatest to the least of them" (Jon. 3:5). Who could possibly have seen that coming?

> Turn your *never* into a *now*, and watch your Nineveh burst open with eternal possibilities.

Turn your *no* into a *yes*, and see what kinds of miracles are waiting on the other side of it. Turn your *never* into a *now*, and watch your Nineveh burst open with eternal possibilities.

Jesus answered, "If anyone loves me,
he will keep my word. My Father will love him,
and we will come to him and make our home with him."
JOHN 14:23 CSB

— He Speaks to Me —

Has God been calling you toward a Nineveh? Instead of listing your objections, list the opportunities.

Be careful to do as the LORD your God has commanded you;
you are not to turn aside to the right or the left.
DEUTERONOMY 5:32 CSB

Blessed are those who hear the word of God and keep it.
LUKE 11:28 CSB

Tailor-Made

*"To him the doorkeeper opens, and the sheep hear his voice,
and he calls his own sheep by name and leads them out."*
JOHN 10:3

A s a second-born daughter with an older sister, my wardrobe as a child was almost exclusively comprised of hand-me-downs. As soon as I was big enough to fit into a dress or a pair of shoes that my sister had outgrown, those articles of clothing became mine—new to *me*—as if they'd come right off the rack in a pretty package.

But by the time I reached a certain age, the "new" had worn off this secondhand, hand-me-down ritual. My sense of style and fashion taste had developed to the point where I desired a wider range of options than just the few pre-worn choices that were available. I was still grateful for the repurposed clothes; I still wore them and liked them and benefited from having them. But I also wanted something that had been shopped for and picked out especially for *me*. I wanted clothes that were *mine*, not always somebody else's. Second-hand clothes had been fine for a while, but now I wanted something tailor-made, specifically selected with me in mind.

When God reveals His Word and will to our pastors, teachers, parents, and others in spiritual authority over us, and they impart those messages to us, we are blessed and should be grateful for their wisdom and instruction. How good of God to multiply what He's given to others so that even we can be blessed by it. And yet we should not become overly dependent. The sign of spiritual maturing and growth is that we should crave personal encounters with God's Spirit that He addresses specifically to us, designed to give us tailor-made, handpicked, personal direction and guidance, hemmed in and firmly rooted in the Scriptures.

In John 10, Jesus pictured the way He intends to relate to us. He is the Good Shepherd—He leads His flock from pasture to pasture, calling to them, caring for them. *All* of them. But even in speaking where they all can hear Him, He also calls them "by name." He knows what each one needs; He know what's specific to His individual sheep. He is intentional and personal, wanting *us* to hear His voice, to follow and obey Him personally.

> Even in speaking where we all can hear Him, He also calls us "by name."

The hand-me-downs are fine and good. We are instructed and discipled by them. We'd be worse off without them. But among the many rights and privileges we enjoy as Christ's followers is the blessing of hearing His voice, one on one. Custom-made for every child in the family. No matter your personality, weakness, deficiencies, or background, the Good Shepherd knows where you are, loves you as His own, and knows how to speak so that you can hear and know where He is leading you.

Personally.

I will stand on my guard post and station myself on the rampart; and I will keep watch to see what He will speak to me.
HABAKKUK 2:1

— He Speaks to Me —

As you read God's Word today, don't just read. Listen. Write down what you hear. It's yours . . . from Him . . .

I, the LORD, will answer them Myself,
as the God of Israel I will not forsake them.
ISAIAH 41:17

You are Christ's body, and individually members of it.
1 CORINTHIANS 12:27

Ball's in Your Court

❀

*I heard the voice of the Lord, saying, "Whom shall I send, and
who will go for Us?" Then I said, "Here am I. Send me!"*
Isaiah 6:8

The girls on my junior high volleyball team were nothing if
not eager, out there in our red and white uniforms, pre-
tending to be as good as other more experienced and well-
coached teams. The ball would come sailing over the net into our
territory, and we'd clasp our hands for action. Several of us who
were closest to where the ball's trajectory was carrying it would
call out in unison, "I've got it! I've got it!"—ready to ignite the
chain reaction of a classic bump-set-spike rhythm. But far too
often, each of us ringing out "I've got it!" would then decide that
one of the other girls, one of our other teammates, probably had
it. So we stepped aside and the ball would thud untouched to the
floor, each of us standing there, watching.

Nobody got it.

"Who will go?" the Lord said to Isaiah. And if we're actively
listening for His voice today, it's what the Lord is still saying to
us in our churches and Bible study groups, or in the middle of
a busy morning, or amid the rustling of His Spirit through the
pages and prayers of our quiet time. And though we sense the
trajectory of His calling coming our direction, and sometimes
bellow out an impressive "I got it!"—so that others around can
hear—we often end up stepping back in hopes that someone else
will step in. Surely another person is better positioned to take on
this task. More qualified, better prepared, better trained, more
adept at handling a mission like this. Surely someone else is the
kind of man or woman who best fits what God wants done here.

We step aside. And the ball of divine mission comes crashing down.

If the Father allows you to see a need, and He softens your heart to be tender toward it, this is your opportunity to engage. It's your invitation to respond and join in His work. Don't step back. Don't recoil. This ball is for you. Who's the person, what's the problem, and where is the deficit that you might be suited to fill? Don't just think about getting it, talk about getting it, or circle in close proximity to it while making half-hearted promises you really don't intend to keep. Like Isaiah (who himself felt uniquely unqualified for such a spiritual assignment), yell "Here am I." *I've got it.*

And then . . . *go get it!*

Is the course of a specific need or ministry opportunity moving into your immediate view? Can you tell the ball is coming into your court? Then it probably means the time for action is now. Clasp your hands, set your feet, and go for it.

Clasp your hands, set your feet, and go for it.

The LORD came and stood and called as at other times, "Samuel! Samuel!" And Samuel said, "Speak, for Your servant is listening."
1 SAMUEL 3:10

— He Speaks to Me —

How has God been tugging on your heart to serve Him in a specific way? How can you actively respond?

As each one has received a special gift, employ it in serving one another as good stewards of the manifold grace of God.
1 PETER 4:10

Even the Son of Man did not come to be served,
but to serve, and to give His life a ransom for many.
MARK 10:45

The Blessing of Pain

*We rejoice in our sufferings, knowing that
suffering produces endurance, and endurance
produces character, and character produces hope.*
ROMANS 5:3–4 ESV

CIP (congenital insensitivity to pain) is an extremely rare medical condition that renders its victims unable to feel pain. Seems a blessing at first—no pain, no hurting, no suffering. And yet the absence of pain inevitably spirals into more harm than good. Without it, an individual is unaware of having a wound that needs tending. They are ignorant of impending danger that could scald their skin, pierce their flesh, or even sever a limb. The pressure is too heavy, the heat too scalding, the cold too freezing, but because the person can't feel it, they unwittingly ignore it, running the real risk of severe, continuing damage.

We may not *like* pain. But we need it. It helps us. Blesses us. It takes us to points of desperation and need (and therefore to pivotal moments of prayer and rescue) that we would never experience if left to our own comfortable routines.

Without the painful emptiness of a barren womb, for example, Hannah might not have called out to God from her distress and her "bitterness of soul" (1 Sam. 1:10 NKJV), receiving the miraculous answer to her prayer that resulted in the birth of Samuel, one of the greatest leaders in all of Israel's history. Without the pain of a heart frayed by the loss of his family, health, and livelihood, Job might never have said to the Lord, "I had heard of you by the hearing of the ear, but now my eye sees you" (Job 42:5 ESV). Without the weeping, wailing, and anguish experienced by the prophet Jeremiah, he might never have known of a "balm in Gilead" (Jer. 8:22).

Stephen, snapping like a twig under the pelting of rocks thrown by the hands of his accusers, "gazed intently into heaven and saw the glory of God" (Acts 7:55). Paul and Silas, shackled to the walls of a Roman jail, with their backs freshly bruised from being thrashed and beaten for their faith, discovered what the true joy of "praying and singing hymns of praise to God" is all about (Acts 16:25). Only through pain could they experience the depths of true worship.

The pain our hearts instinctively avoid while striving for endless happiness and comfort is actually a mysterious blessing. It compels us to more accurately assess the wisdom or foolishness of our choices. It forces us to seek refuge in God that we might otherwise think is unnecessary. It becomes a teacher exposing us to lessons that only the hurting can understand. Pain is ironically the key to being spared even worse discomfort. Because when we feel it, we make beneficial, needful adjustments.

> Pain is ironically the key to being spared even worse discomfort.

So perhaps this would be a good day to thank your loving heavenly Father for blessing you with the gift of pain. Heaven knows where we'd be without it.

*No discipline seems enjoyable at the time, but painful.
Later on, however, it yields the peaceful fruit of
righteousness to those who have been trained by it.*
HEBREWS 12:11 CSB

— He Speaks to Me —

How are you hurting the most acutely today? What adjustments should you make in response to it? How should it inform and enhance how you relate to God? What growth are you experiencing because of it?

_The LORD is near to the brokenhearted and
saves those who are crushed in spirit._
PSALM 34:18

Just as the sufferings of Christ are ours in abundance,
so also our comfort is abundant through Christ.
2 Corinthians 1:5

Divine Disguise

---

*I consider that the sufferings of this present time
are not worth comparing with the glory that is going
to be revealed to us. For the creation eagerly waits
with anticipation for God's sons to be revealed.*
ROMANS 8:18–19 CSB

I was elbow-deep in dirty dishes when her image appeared on the television screen. A svelte woman, clad in sleek, tight-fitting athletic gear, racing like a gazelle through her morning exercise. Her ponytail bounced in rhythm with her pounding strides upon the pavement, as a single tear of sweat ran dramatically down her temple toward her chiseled jaw line. Lean. Swift. Powerful. Beautiful. I was spellbound.

"There's an athlete among us," the deep commercial voice-over intoned, as thirty seconds of envy dripped from my sudsy, rubber-gloved fingertips. Yes, "there's an athlete among us," he said . . . "disguised as a wife and mother."

Ahhh. *Disguised.* She changed diapers and cleaned dishes and washed clothes. But none of that negated the fact that she was also something more.

What's *your* role or occupation? Wife? Mother? Executive? Manager? Single woman? Ministry director? Friend? Widow? Grandmother? Those are each significant things to be and do. And yet they are not, in and of themselves, the sum total of *who you are.* They are only your divine disguise . . . the veneer around "the new self who is being renewed to a true knowledge according to the image of the One who created" you (Col. 3:10). Underneath it all, you are a Christ-follower imbued with the presence of God. You are part of a royal priesthood who's been redeemed, set free, and gifted to fulfill His purposes for you on the earth. You are not just a woman who works and leads and often cleans up from the same supper she also invested a good hour or more in preparing. You are a participant in the plan of God on this planet.

The roles we play, and to which we've been called, are important. So we fulfill them with all of the faith, hard work, and commitment that God's Spirit musters in us. But we must continually remember that these roles don't tell everything about who we are, or about the power plant of spiritual vitality God has placed inside us for being the kind of person who is on heaven's assignment.

> Underneath it all, you are a Christ-follower imbued with the presence of God.

All of creation wants to see that woman "revealed"—released, unveiled, turned loose. The ordinary tasks that come along with your roles in this season of life are not merely chores to be endured. They are opportunities for a disciplined, determined daughter of God to transform them into activities brimming with eternal meaning and purpose.

Wonder what this day, in fact, might reveal about you.

If you belong to Christ, then you are
Abraham's descendants, heirs according to promise.
GALATIANS 3:29

— He Speaks to Me —

How would your choices and attitudes shift if you saw your roles and responsibilities not as restrictions but as openings for God to be seen through you?

Beloved, now we are children of God,
and it has not appeared as yet what we will be.
1 John 3:2

*He chose us in Him before the foundation of the world,
that we would be holy and blameless before Him.*
EPHESIANS 1:4

Imperfectly Satisfied

※

*We know that if the earthly tent which is our house
is torn down, we have a building from God,
a house not made with hands, eternal in the heavens.*
2 CORINTHIANS 5:1

A sliver of imperfection runs through everything and every-one we come across in this world. Even those things we hope will perfectly satisfy us—our dream house, our dream car, our dream job, our dream husband—will each show signs of age, wear, and depreciation over time. Their flaws and weaknesses eventually become exposed, revealing an ever-present need for upkeep, reworking, and repair.

What's more, we ourselves prove no different. As our body advances through the years, gravity tugs against even our best attempts at maintaining the tone and firmness that once seemed to come so naturally.

We wish this reality weren't the case. But it is. Every plea-sure we enjoy will at some point, and in some way, fall short of what we desire. Nothing can be our *everything* because, in some way, it will leave us wanting and needing and thirsting for more. And as our wishes for longer-lasting durability are repeatedly dashed and disappointed, we often find ourselves longing for something better . . . for something that is truly, unendingly perfect and eternal.

This is what life's imperfections are supposed to do—make us long for something otherworldly. It's why Earth's flaws actu-ally end up being some of God's greatest gifts. The lost ideal of Eden, marred beyond recognition by human sin, means that nothing in this world can ever be misconstrued as whole and incorruptible. The quest for perfection will always be beyond our grasp. Unattainable in time and space. So we'll need to look elsewhere.

We'll need to look upward.

The gnawing frustration and dissatisfaction we feel should become our most prized guides, stirring our spiritual hunger and leading us toward perfection, toward the only *perfect One.* They should grab our hands and hearts and lead us to eagerly hunger for God and eternity. They should make us long for the stability of "a building from God, a house not made with hands, eternal in the heavens."

So when you see the ding in your pristine passenger door, the snag on your new jacket from which the tags still hang, the chip on the face of your cell phone, the creaking board in the staircase, or the character flaw in your best friend, remember—the fault that frustrates you, the error that discourages you, the defect that makes you want something more: they each serve as divine antagonists, stirring your heart for something else, for Someone who will never falter, *never*, at *any* time, especially not at the *worst possible* time.

> Allow life's imperfections to become everyday signs that point you to Jesus.

Allow life's imperfections to become what they were always meant to be—everyday signs that point you to Jesus. Use them as your cues that encourage you to look up from the annoyances of earthly life and see Him. The only One who truly satisfies.

They desire a better country, that is,
a heavenly one. Therefore God is not ashamed to
be called their God; for He has prepared a city for them.
HEBREWS 11:16

— He Speaks to Me —

List the things that have left you feeling unsatisfied lately. How do these imperfections point you to Jesus?

If you have been raised up with Christ, keep seeking the things above, where Christ is, seated at the right hand of God.
Colossians 3:1

Store up for yourselves treasures in heaven, where neither moth nor rust destroys, and where thieves do not break in or steal.
Matthew 6:20

Ticketed Passengers Only

✤

Jesus said to him, "I am the way, and the truth, and the life;
no one comes to the Father but through Me."
JOHN 14:6

Soon after confirming this man was in my seat—by checking my boarding pass against the numbers on the cabin compartment—I realized I'd seen his face before. He was somebody famous (I knew that), I just wasn't sure who he was or what world I was supposed to know him from. Movies? TV news? Tech genius? Retired football star? All I knew for sure, from the way he was calmly reading his newspaper, was that he either wasn't aware he was sitting in my seat or, perhaps more likely, didn't care.

My sports-fanatic husband, however, who was queuing up behind me in the tight airplane aisle, took only a second to recognize this man as a Hall of Fame, former NBA basketball coach. Which was sort of exciting, of course, to be an arm's length distance from someone who'd roamed the sidelines with some of the all-time greats. But still . . .

He was in my seat.

When Jerry gingerly brought this point to his attention, the gentleman reached into his pants pocket, drew out a creased ticket, and silently noted the discrepancy through his reading glasses. His surprised expression said it all. He apologetically gathered his belongings, flashed an embarrassed grin, and kindly patted me on the shoulder as he scooted away to locate his correctly assigned accommodations.

Because no matter who he was, what he'd accomplished, or how much fame he had accrued, he didn't have a ticket for this seat.

Generation after generation, many have sought to ensure their eternal seat assignment based on what they've accomplished in life. Some have grown accustomed to having most any seat they have wanted because of their success and prestige, or simply their everyday track record of being well-regarded, well-respected, and well-behaved. They can't imagine they've caused enough trouble in life to cost them entrance into heaven.

Yet on that great and fearful day when the trumpet of the Lord sounds, no one's résumés and lists of achievements will be read, admired, and consulted for making seating decisions. Nothing we're able to pull from our pocket of personal goodness will serve as a suitable pass. Only our believing faith (or lack of faith) in the Son of God will factor into what happens next. And many will be left standing with nowhere to rest their laurels.

Many will be left standing with nowhere to rest their laurels.

It is only Christ's righteousness applied to our sinful hearts that guarantees our placement in heavenly places. So I ask you, does His name appear on your ticket? Be sure you know the answer before you go to bed tonight.

There is salvation in no one else; for there is no other name under heaven that has been given among men by which we must be saved.
Acts 4:12

— He Speaks to Me —

Have you, even inadvertently, depended on anything or anyone to assure you entrance into heaven other than a relationship with Jesus Christ?

The righteousness of God is through faith in Jesus Christ to all who believe, since there is no distinction.
ROMANS 3:22 CSB

*Let the one who is thirsty come; let the one who
wishes take the water of life without cost.*
REVELATION 22:17

Treasures Worth Keeping

———————— ⚜ ————————

Mary treasured all these things,
pondering them in her heart.
Luke 2:19

We have lost the art of *treasuring*.

In a day when such abundance and prosperity abound, when every sort of gift and gadget can be ours with little more than a few clicks of online action, we no longer know what it means to truly value a keepsake. Things (even people) have become disposable, expendable, easily replaced with a different model if they happen to break or just don't work out like we wanted. Lose it, and we can always get another, probably with two-day delivery thrown in for free.

So we don't prize particular things or place significant worth on precious items, not the way folks once did. We're not as careful to protect, nurture, and preserve them, taking great care with their condition, being sure we're tending to their regular upkeep.

And while this may or may not be a tragic loss to our age in history, it's certainly a grave issue whenever this same, lethargic posture leaks over into our relationship with God.

Perhaps we're faithful in reading His Word. Perhaps we're prayerful in listening for His voice. But if we don't treasure the results of these exchanges with Him—if we don't see our personal interactions as irreplaceable keepsakes to be held and pondered and handled with care—we'll squander what He is so good to give us. If we aren't careful to note the Spirit's personal conviction to us, whether from our pastor's message or our personal quiet time—if we don't carve out time and space for keeping a record of the web of events where we can trace His handiwork in our lives—the moments slip away forgotten. Life covers them over. A month later, we can't even remember. The details that were so fresh one day are now forgotten treasure.

We've grown too casual with the holy.

I don't know exactly what Mary, the mother of Jesus, did to treasure the happenings in her son's life. But the original wording that comes down to us as "treasured" in Luke 2:19 implies a defending, a preserving, a protecting of those memories. She was determined not to merely be awestruck and amazed by it all, the way others were, in general, when "all who heard it wondered at the things which were told them" (v. 18). Instead, she took it a step further, valiantly keeping and guarding the account. These memories were worth tucking away, preserving, remembering. They were worthy of safekeeping and appreciating. They were, after all, about Jesus.

> We've grown too casual with the holy.

Every instance in which we detect the fingerprints of God orchestrating and intervening, every time we hear the weighty whisper of the Holy Spirit echoing in our hearts, we ought to be quick to preserve those happenings so they cannot be easily forgotten.

Mary didn't treat something (Someone) of such value carelessly. These words and works of the Son of God were (and are) worth treasuring.

The grass withers, the flower fades,
but the word of our God stands forever.
ISAIAH 40:8

— He Speaks to Me —

Utilize this devotional as your treasure box. What might you want to record inside for safe keeping?

In him are hidden all the treasures of wisdom and knowledge.
COLOSSIANS 2:3 CSB

For where your treasure is, there your heart will be also.
MATTHEW 6:21

Even There

While they were there, the days were
completed for her to give birth.
LUKE 2:6

Caesar Augustus emerged from a period of shared rule to become the first Roman emperor, where he governed with godlike acclaim in the decades leading up to Jesus' birth. If you don't know him from the history books, you know him from the Christmas story: "In those days a decree went out from Caesar Augustus, that a census should be taken of all the inhabited earth" (Luke 2:1). All citizens were commanded to return to the place of their birth to be counted and taxed in order that the emperor would receive the wealth, power, and complete control he desired for himself.

Such self-serving, even secular reasoning from him.

And such terrible timing for her.

Mary was full-term pregnant with the Messiah when she likely half walked, half rode on some kind of burden-bearing animal for eighty or ninety miles from Nazareth to Bethlehem. It was a miserable journey. The slow, rolling gait was brutal on her heavily expecting frame, as well as on her troubled mind, as she traveled the dusty path, knowing the possibility was high that she might end up giving birth far from the safety and familiarity of home.

As the labor pains began to press in, she found herself not only in an unfamiliar town but in accommodations more suitable for animals than humans. And "while they were there," the Bible says, in this unsavory place, "the days were completed for her to give birth." While *there*.

She was aware, of course, that the child she was carrying was the Son of God, that "He will reign over the house of Jacob forever, and His kingdom will have no end" (Luke 1:33). Yet I'm curious if she recalled, or had ever been told, that one of the prophets of Scripture had spoken of Bethlehem as the birthplace of this soon coming king. We can't be sure. We only know from the biblical record that uncomfortable and undesirable circumstances had put her *there*—displaced, and yet perfectly placed, all at once.

Do not be discouraged today if you, too, are *there*—in a loveless marriage, at an underwhelming job, in a difficult ministry, in an uncomfortable town, discarded from that long-term friendship or what you hoped to be a lifetime relationship. Even *there* God can do miraculous things in you, and through you, and all for His glory. He can align this timing and placement with His sovereign and preplanned purposes. He can stun you in hindsight when you discover the careful orchestration of events in your life. What He intends to accomplish—the thing that most bears the fingerprints of His Spirit—cannot be thwarted.

> Even *there* God can do miraculous things in you.

Rest. Trust. He has not forgotten you. Not then, not now. Not here, not *there*.

There is an appointed time for everything.
And there is a time for every event under heaven.
ECCLESIASTES 3:1

— He Speaks to Me —

Where's your "there"? Submit this divine placement to God, and ask Him to reveal His purposes for you while you are positioned there.

_____

_____

_____

_____

_____

_____

_____

_____

_____

_____

_____

_____

The mind of man plans his way,
but the LORD directs his steps.
PROVERBS 16:9

*In God, whose word I praise, in God I have put my trust;
I shall not be afraid. What can mere man do to me?*
PSALM 56:4

Life: The Edited Version

He will sit as a smelter and purifier of silver, and He will purify the sons of Levi and refine them like gold and silver, so that they may present to the LORD offerings in righteousness.
MALACHI 3:3

*M*y writings usually come back from my editor with one specific note: "It's too long." *Too long?* But everything I put into the manuscript had a reason, had a place. And when the edited version arrives in my in-box, I'm shocked at what has been taken out. In my opinion, the portions he has deleted were crucial to what I was trying to say. Without them, the book has lost its cutting edge. But the editor, the expert, explains: "If it's too long, you'll lose the reader's attention. You'll dampen the impact and usefulness of your words. Cutting it down will add to its value. Trust me. I know what I'm doing."

Hesitantly, I submit.

The divine Editor does this very thing with the version of our lives that we each present to Him—cutting, shaving, dicing, carving—until it communicates most clearly the message He wants to bring out of it. And of us.

The design we dreamed up took weeks, months, years to arrange. We based its narrative on desires and plans that we're certain will ensure our happiness, complete with a classic story-book ending. We've included details about our education, our family, our friends, our finances, our ministry involvement, our reputation for all the ways we live out our service to Him. He should *love* this, should be floored by its full, rich storyline and how we intend it all as a way of praising Him. It's got everything. It's perfect.

Taking out the red pen of His grace, He scratches through a number of plot lines, ambitions, and relationships that will prove detrimental to the direction He knows my story needs to go. Then He rewrites many busy tasks and frantic religious activities until they look more like solitude, stillness, and silence. My plans for finances and family have also been reworked to include less concern about what kinds of possessions we own, what kinds of clothes we wear, what kinds of image we send off to others. His rewritten text shows that my loved ones can be comfortable with much less extravagance than I anticipated.

> Cutting it down will add to its value.

It all looks so different now. Most of the original themes behind each chapter have been changed. All-new priorities have been penciled in. Even the title I'd given it—*My Life*—has been redrawn with the subhead, *The Edited Version.*

I push back against these cuts, these deletions. But He is kind. He whispers: "Daughter, if your story is too full, it will lose its purpose. Cutting it down will add to its value. Trust Me. I know what I'm doing."

Hesitantly, yet somehow sure He's right, I submit to my Editor . . . again.

Godliness actually is a means of great gain when accompanied by contentment. For we have brought nothing into the world, so we cannot take anything out of it either.
1 TIMOTHY 6:6–7

— He Speaks to Me —

How do you typically respond to the Father's "edits" on your life? And why?

_____

_____

_____

_____

_____

_____

_____

_____

_____

_____

_____

_____

Better is a little with the fear of the L<small>ORD</small>
than great treasure and turmoil with it.
P<small>ROVERBS</small> 15:16

The end of the matter; all has been heard. Fear God and keep his commandments, for this is the whole duty of man.
ECCLESIASTES 12:13 ESV

— Day 27 —

Daily Bread

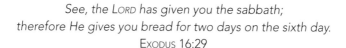

See, the LORD has given you the sabbath;
therefore He gives you bread for two days on the sixth day.
EXODUS 16:29

God gave the newly freed Israelites food every morning throughout their long journey—food they didn't farm or cultivate or need to go to the market and buy. They just walked out of their tents at break of day, and there it was—sparkling clear on the ground. *Manna.* "The bread of angels," the Bible calls it (Ps. 78:25). Sweet, luscious, and free. And remarkably filling and versatile.

But on the sixth day of each week, God layered a double portion of manna into the morning supply, not only giving the people enough to carry them and their families through the next day, but also giving them that seventh day off from the work of gleaning. The Sabbath was the margin in their weekly routine that was meant to remain dedicated to Him—the boundary around His blessing—a gift of rest to slaves who had never experienced rest in their entire lives. Yahweh promised them that if they would honor this margin, He would make certain they would always have enough. More importantly, they would always be reminded that He alone was their source.

And yet when the seventh day rolled around, "some of the people went out to gather" anyway (Exod. 16:27).

Why did they do this? More personally, why do *we*? We're constantly gathering and producing and spending and eating and collecting and keeping and hoarding—beyond what we should, beyond what we need—instead of genuinely enjoying and appreciating what God has already done, instead of trusting that He is our ultimate provider and will sustain us when we honor His boundaries. Like ancient Israel, we tend to overextend, reaching into the margins in our calendar, pilfering from spaces that should be reserved and untouchable, not giving ourselves opportunity to reflect on His goodness, opportunity to remember that He is our ruler, not our own strength and resources.

Sabbath was not meant as a complication in the Israelites' lives, a hurdle to be worked around each week. Sabbath was (and is) a gift from God—a pause, a stopping point, a decision to take a break from going and buying and doing and accruing. It is the Spirit-empowered choice to cease striving and enjoy our God. It is the margin that reminds us He is in full control. It is the peace that comes in the midst of all that whirlwind and flurry of activity. Sabbath is what beats our lives into submission, giving us the breathing room for getting our sanity back.

> **Sabbath was (and is) a gift from God.**

We cannot afford to neglect the Sabbath principle.

Stop the madness. Break the mind-numbing cycle. Rest and receive this beautiful gift from Him. With open hands, and with open hearts, let us remember and receive the gift of our freedom.

The gift of Sabbath margin.

Make sure that your character is free from the love of money, being content with what you have; for He Himself has said, "I will never desert you, nor will I ever forsake you."
HEBREWS 13:5

— He Speaks to Me —

What would "Sabbath margin" look like in your calendar? In your children's calendar? In your living space? In your work space?

_____

_____

_____

_____

_____

_____

_____

_____

_____

_____

_____

_____

Blessed be the LORD, who has given rest to
His people Israel, according to all that He promised;
not one word has failed of all His good promise.
1 KINGS 8:56

Rest in the LORD and wait patiently for Him.
PSALM 37:7

Table Talk

*So the woman went her way and ate,
and her face was no longer sad.*
1 Samuel 1:18

If you've lost your hunger for life, love, and joy—if you're marked today by fatigue, depression, and weakness—if you feel little interest in things that used to interest you the most—an Old Testament woman can show you how to get your appetite back.

Hannah was in despair. Her rival wife was bearing children for their shared husband as fast as she could conceive them. Yet Hannah suffered along silently in her barrenness. Constantly berated by the other woman's provocations and catty remarks, Hannah came to the point of being so distraught, she didn't even feel like eating (v. 7).

Maybe you've been there, feeling *that* upset. Maybe you *are* there—burdened by dashed hopes, lost love, crippled dreams, ailing health, or debilitating difficulty and trauma. Not even your favorite foods could tempt you. Not now. But things changed for Hannah . . . giving us hope that they can change for us all as well.

The family took their annual pilgrimage to Shiloh, where the house of the Lord was located. And while there, "greatly distressed," Hannah "prayed to the Lord and wept bitterly" (v. 10). Her desire for a child was so deep and extreme that she vowed to relinquish this yet preconceived son to the Lord as an offering of thanks, dedicating his life into the service of God and God's people. Her prayer was so intense and passionate, the Bible says, that Eli the priest mistook her for a drunken woman.

But finally, with her heart completely poured out before God, something remarkable happened.

God gave Hannah her appetite back.

Despite her prayer yet to be answered.

Despite her cruel sister-wife's ruthless taunting.

Despite her husband's naïve insensitivity to her condition.

Nothing had changed the tiniest bit in any of her pitiful circumstances. Yet after offloading her tears and frustrations at God's feet, she "went her way and ate, and her face was no longer sad."

Amazing what calling out on the Lord can accomplish.

The power of prayer can work wonders—not only in your spiritual life, but also in your physical, practical well-being. All the way down inside you. He can give you your hunger back—for food, for family, for work, for ministry. For life.

> You satisfy me as with rich food;
> my mouth will praise you with joyful lips.
> PSALM 63:5 CSB

— He Speaks to Me —

Pour our your heart to the Lord. Admit the areas where you are lacking a healthy appetite, and ask Him to give you your hunger back.

Is anyone among you suffering? He should pray.
Is anyone cheerful? He should sing praises.
JAMES 5:13 CSB

Everyone who exalts himself will be humbled,
but he who humbles himself will be exalted.
Luke 18:14

Of Fractions and Fullness

*We cared so much for you that we were pleased to share with
you not only the gospel of God but also our own lives.*
1 THESSALONIANS 2:8 CSB

Multiplication is a mathematical operation that generally results in putting numbers together to make them bigger. We think of multiplication in terms of growth. Three apples times five children equals fifteen apples altogether. Larger outcomes. Expanding products. But when you multiply any whole number by a *fraction*, an inverse result takes place. The answer is actually *smaller* than the whole number in the equation. Combining fractions into a multiplication problem takes *away* from its value, rather than contributing *more* to it.

And despite what people say about how we never use the things we learn in school in real life, certain math principles do come with applications that convert into everyday experience.

We see it taking place in the life of Paul. His ministry to the church at Thessalonica didn't last long, apparently only a few weeks (Acts 17:2). Yet even his brief stay caused enough of an uproar that his Christian brothers had to hustle him and his ministry companion Silas out of town under cover of darkness (v. 10) to avoid being caught up in the riot. But in that thin space of time, Paul gave himself completely to the task—expanding, increasing, and multiplying their growth. He not only "reasoned with them from the Scriptures" (v. 2), teaching them sound doctrine of the faith, but he did what he always did in every place where he ministered. He dove into those relationships with both feet, putting himself at their full disposal, loving and investing in them without any reservation. Not in fractions, withholding portions for later. But wholly and fully. Whatever it cost. Whatever they needed.

He was all-in. One hundred percent committed to the task. To the people. To his friends. This investment yielded a bountiful harvest in the life of the church.

"Having so fond an affection for you," he wrote to them later, "we were well-pleased to impart to you not only the gospel of God but also our own lives"—their own *lives*—"because you had become very dear to us. For you recall, brethren, our labor and hardship, how working night and day so as not to be a burden to any of you, we proclaimed to you the gospel of God" (1 Thess. 2:8–9). He spent those few weeks there "exhorting and encouraging and imploring" them, the way "a father would his own children" (v. 11), totally focused on helping them "walk in a manner worthy of the God who calls you into His own kingdom and glory" (v. 12).

Here's to being whole-number people.

Expansion. Multiplication. Growth. For the glory of God.

What kind of friend, spouse, son, daughter, employee, or team member are you? Are you the type who brings your wholehearted determination and investment into these various relationships? Or do you hold back, only devoting a fractional, half effort into the mix, not really making yourself available and vulnerable and invested in growing the people around you?

Here's to being whole-number people, the kinds of women and men who encourage fuller, deeper, healthier, more bountiful results in every relationship and encounter and effort that is entrusted to us. May we cause vast multiplication—expanding joy, peace, and the power of our God—everywhere we go.

Having purified your souls by your obedience to the truth for a sincere brotherly love, love one another earnestly from a pure heart.
1 Peter 1:22 esv

— He Speaks to Me —

What are the relationships and endeavors that the Lord is asking you to fully invest in?

One person gives freely, yet gains more;
another withholds what is right, only to become poor.
PROVERBS 11:24 CSB

I will most gladly spend and be expended for your souls.
2 Corinthians 12:15

One-Track Mind

🦋
---

*"I glorified You on the earth, having accomplished
the work which You have given Me to do."*
JOHN 17:4

The pressures experienced by Jesus during His human life-span were unfathomable. We know from Scripture only a small portion of the demands placed on Him by those who either wanted Him to demonstrate His power more prolifically, more personally, or who were looking for some angle to exploit what He could do. Each day, each night, came with steady drips of pressure, often jetting from multiple places all at once, trying to pressure Him into conforming to whatever mold would meet someone else's particular time line, purpose, or agenda.

He chose not to indulge most of these self-styled challenges and requests—not because He was uncompassionate or unaware of the genuine need around Him, but because He was here on assignment. He arrived with a specific job to do, a mission that was being set up and carried out with each new decision He made within each new hour He'd been allotted. So instead of being swayed by the whims and requests of the masses, instead of allowing others to drive His progress and priorities, the Son diligently asked the Father what *His* assignment entailed for Him in that moment, and then He stuck to that plan and did only those things the Father showed Him.

Yes, even Jesus—who (unlike us) could do *everything*—didn't *do* everything. He only did the things assigned to Him. The divinely delegated things that were His to complete.

That's why even after such a brief, concentrated period of personal ministry, He could legitimately make a statement of fact we so often wish we could make ourselves. "I glorified You on the earth," He said to His Father, "having accomplished the work which You have given Me to do."

How many times, in all your overwhelmed, overextended perplexity, have you fantasized about jotting the final checkmark on your lengthy list of items to complete, collapsing comfortably into bed, looking up past the nicely dusted ceiling fan twirling above you, and whispering contently, "It's finished. Everything you wanted done today, Lord, I did it."

Jesus, who (unlike us) could do everything, didn't.

Jesus, bearing a mission load more gigantic and self-sacrificial than any we can possibly comprehend . . . did it. Everything the Father wanted of Him. And nothing else. He "accomplished the work" He'd been given to do, because He'd avoided falling victim to the tyranny of the urgent.

We won't be flawless in the execution. We can never be as completely disciplined as Jesus, able to tune out all things that might distract us from our straight-ahead objective. But there are choices we can make by His Spirit. There are requests we can say no to. There are expectations we can manage. And there are specific assignments we can maximize by staying on task and on purpose, no matter how hard life pulls us in the opposite direction.

Let your eyes look directly ahead
and let your gaze be fixed straight in front of you.
PROVERBS 4:25

— He Speaks to Me —

What do you think the Father is asking of you today? How can you streamline your commitments in order to honor your God-assignment?

Forgetting what lies behind and reaching forward
to what lies ahead, I press on toward the goal for
the prize of the upward call of God in Christ Jesus.
PHILIPPIANS 3:13–14

We know that the Son of God has come and has given
us understanding so that we may know the true one.
1 JOHN 5:20 CSB

Go and Look

❀

He said to them, "How many loaves do you have? Go look!"
And when they found out, they said, "Five, and two fish."
MARK 6:38

"What's wrong?" I asked my youngest son, even though I already knew the answer. I rubbed his cheek lightly with the back of my hand, lifting his chin upward so he could look me in the eye.

"I'm bored," he responded glumly. "There's nothing for me to play with."

"Really?" I said. "Absolutely nothing?" I tilted my head to one side, staring back at him with a questioning expression. "Sure you can't find *anything*? Why don't you go and look?". . . because as many times as I've felt that same sense of deprivation, I've heard God's voice echoing from a distant Galilean shoreline, saying to His disciples those words that refused to let them off the hook so easily, "How many loaves do you have? Go look!"

The Twelve looked out over the vast, hungry multitude and determined that this problem they'd been presented with solving was much too big for them to manage. They were in a desolate patch of ground on the outskirts of town. There were no merchants or vendors in the area to offer food for the people. In the disciples' estimation, there was nothing here to work with. Not even enough to play with.

But then, Jesus—"Go. Look."

What they found was nothing more than a child's lunch. No, it wasn't much maybe. But it was all they needed. This meager meal would be plenty to satiate the crowd who were scattered about them, once Jesus got His hands on it, once He started breaking bread into full servings that had them tossing the uneaten scraps back into each disciple's basket. Once Jesus became involved, people couldn't hold another bite. The only thing His disciples had needed to do was stop pointing to what they didn't have and discover what they did.

So I ask you—same as I asked my son, same as God's Spirit has often asked me—"Have you really taken time to go and look?" Or are you simply complaining about what you think you're missing? If you're sure you're out of options, if you're certain the supplies on hand are nothing compared to the resources He's made available to someone else, chances are you've not taken a second look at what's already at your disposal. Ask the Lord to open your spiritual eyes to see how much raw material He's provided for you to utilize in fulfilling His purposes for this moment. Don't discount the little things. They can become blessed things if you'll go back and look at them through the lens of divine possibility.

Now go.

And look.

> Don't discount the little things. They can become blessed things.

*In any and all circumstances I have learned
the secret of being content—whether well
fed or hungry, whether in abundance or in need.*
PHILIPPIANS 4:12 CSB

— He Speaks to Me —

Go and look again at the areas of your life where you tend to feel the most unsatisfied and discontent. Make a list of what the Lord *has* given you, express your gratitude, and ask Him to shift your perspective.

Young lions lack food and go hungry,
but those who seek the LORD will not lack any good thing.
PSALM 34:10 CSB

What does the Lord require of you but to do justice,
to love kindness, and to walk humbly with your God?
Micah 6:8

Watch Your Boat

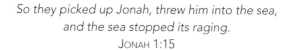

So they picked up Jonah, threw him into the sea,
and the sea stopped its raging.
JONAH 1:15

Most of us have our favorite Bible verses—the ones that comfort us through difficult times, the ones that speak of heavenly promises about the future. We latch onto those (as we should!) and ride them through the turbulent waters of everyday life.

But the Bible is a big-picture book. It covers everything. And while the love and mercy and goodness and grace of God are all true to His nature and accurately descriptive of His heart, His calls for our repentance and to surrendered adjustments in our lifestyle are equally true. Sin is no good for us, and our God knows it—which is why He's included some of our *not* so favorite verses too . . . about His justice, His discipline, His wrath, His awesome and fearful presence. When one of His children chooses willful disobedience, remaining unrepentant, He wants them restored to Him badly enough that He will bare these harder edges of His character as a way of wooing them back to sanity, back into fellowship.

Oftentimes, however, because of the interconnectedness of human relationships, the people nearest to those who are subject to His discipline can feel these tremors of God's action as well. Being in close proximity to people that you know are running from God and are in the crosshairs of His corrective measures can inadvertently put you in the line of fire.

The scenario played out on board an Old Testament boat bound for Tarshish. Jonah was running from God, going *down* to Joppa, going *down* to the ship's hold, going *down* into a deep sleep, soon going *down* into the belly of a great fish. A violent storm rocked that vessel as God sought to get His runaway prophet's attention. But a whole bunch of unsuspecting sailors ended up being affected by the fallout too. The simple seafaring mission they'd planned on taking became a death-defying voyage that cost them their cargo and made them doubt for a long time that they'd ever see dry land again.

This is why you must watch your boat, sailor. Take great care in choosing those you intend to travel any distance with. Whether a business partner, a romantic relationship, or any other kind of binding affiliation that's sure to throw the two of you together and intertwine your personal time and resources, do your best to find out through prayer, conversation, and wise counsel whether or not you're getting into the boat with someone who might be a tidal wave target.

> Being in close proximity to people in the crosshairs of His corrective measures can put you in the line of fire as well.

Sometimes, of course, you can't know—or you're already yoked together with the person (like in marriage, for instance), and must simply ride out the rapids like the sailors in Jonah's story and seek to remedy the problem through whatever biblical means the Lord shows you.

But before you enter another work arrangement or binding contract or serious friendship that seems like it's going somewhere positive, see if their heart is tender toward God and submitted to His way—whether their earnest desire is to honor Him and yield to His will. Because if a storm of discipline is coming in somebody else's life, you don't want to be in the line of fire.

He who walks with wise men will be wise,
but the companion of fools will suffer harm.
PROVERBS 13:20

— He Speaks to Me —

How have you experienced this reality? What can you do differently now to keep from experiencing it again?

Do not be bound together with unbelievers;
for what partnership have righteousness and lawlessness,
or what fellowship has light with darkness?
2 CORINTHIANS 6:14

*If your brother sins, go and show him his fault in private;
if he listens to you, you have won your brother.*
MATTHEW 18:15

Forgiveness in Action

I urge you to reaffirm your love for him . . .
so that no advantage would be taken of us by Satan.
2 CORINTHIANS 2:8, 11

Unforgiveness often feels like a relatively harmless way of dealing with unpleasant circumstances or unpleasant people. It puts up an artificial shell of protection that makes us assume we are shielded from more damage. From our vantage point of self-protection, it appears to be the most advantage posture to maintain. But Paul gives clarity on the demonic origins and damaging outcomes of unforgiveness.

Unforgiveness, he writes, is one of the ways that a Christian is "outwitted by Satan" (2 Cor. 2:11 ESV). It's one of the "designs" or "schemes" or "devices" our Enemy uses to keep us jailed in bitterness, shackled by resentment, crippled from our effectiveness in prayer, and stunted in our power to stand against him victoriously. When our hearts become even slightly hardened by refusing to walk in free and open fellowship with another, we partner with the Enemy in our own internal jailing.

The beloved apostle John adds that anyone who chooses unforgiveness "is in the darkness and walks in the darkness, and does not know where he is going because the darkness has blinded his eyes" (1 John 2:11).

It's no small thing, this unforgiveness.

But perhaps a small yet critical suggestion could incite our complete escape from it. Paul instructed the Corinthians to forgive *actively*—to seal the emotional effort of forgiving with a visible, tangible expression of love to the one who has offended us. It could be only a small overture: a smile given, a meal prepared, a birthday wish offered, a friendly email sent. But when we do it, we deliberately move *toward* freedom instead of hoping it comes looking for us. We shower the offender with a grace they weren't expecting and likely don't deserve. And where they may currently be "overwhelmed" by a level of "excessive sorrow" that we don't even know about (2 Cor. 2:7), whether by the broken relationship they miss sharing with us or by some other circumstance that weighs on them in private, our one little act of gracious generosity may be the nudge that shakes them loose from the stifling bondage of regret, shame, and embarrassment they carry around on their shoulders.

If your skin bristles at the thought of doing something kind for this person who's caused you such pain, your hesitance alone could indicate you're not as in line with forgiveness as you may once have thought. But remember, you're not receiving any benefit by holding back. Instead, by remaining bitter, you're serving the Enemy's purposes, falling prey to his schemes against you.

> It's no small thing, this unforgiveness.

And maybe that little reminder is all you need to encourage you not to let this issue linger on any longer.

So forgive—internally *and also* actively.

If your enemy is hungry, give him food to eat;
and if he is thirsty, give him water to drink.
PROVERBS 25:21

— He Speaks to Me —

Ask the Lord to show you how to thwart Satan's designs by extending kindness to another.

_____

_____

_____

_____

_____

_____

_____

_____

_____

_____

_____

_____

_____

Bless those who persecute you; bless and do not curse.
ROMANS 12:14

Beyond all these things put on love,
which is the perfect bond of unity.
Colossians 3:14

Never Too Far Gone

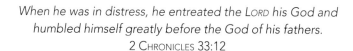

*When he was in distress, he entreated the L*ORD *his God and*
humbled himself greatly before the God of his fathers.
2 CHRONICLES 33:12

To say Manasseh was an evil king is like saying the Grand Canyon is a hole in the ground. The Bible says he "shed so much innocent blood that he filled Jerusalem with it from one end to another" (2 Kings 21:16 CSB). If any one monarch's abominations were to blame for God's abandonment of Judah to exile, it was this king who had "done wickedly more than all the Amorites did who were before him" (2 Chron. 33:11).

Gratefully, God is not a stoic being who deals with humankind in a manner devoid of emotions and sentiments. "The LORD is compassionate and gracious, slow to anger and abounding in lovingkindness. He will not always strive with us, nor will He keep His anger forever. He has not dealt with us according to our sins, nor rewarded us according to our iniquities. For as high as the heavens are above the earth, so great is His lovingkindness toward those who fear Him" (Ps. 103:8–11).

Even when we've chosen unwisely, even when we've relished our stubborn resistance, He remains eager to express these beautiful elements of His character to us. He longs to receive the rebellious back into His welcoming arms. He loves seeing His grace exalted and watching it change us into His image. Nothing we've done, no matter how devastating or devious, can push us too far out of His love to reach us, rescue us, and restore us. When we call to Him, He hears us.

Just like He heard Manasseh . . .

For when the Lord sent the armies of a foreign nation against him, "and they captured Manasseh with hooks, bound him with bronze chains and took him to Babylon" (2 Chron. 33:11), judgment fell like hailstones. But in his distress, Manasseh "humbled himself greatly" (v. 12) before the Lord. And God "was moved by his entreaty and heard his supplication, and brought him again to Jerusalem to his kingdom" (v. 13). After such bountiful restoration, Manasseh received his kingdom back, and the remainder of his life (vv. 14–16) looked a whole lot different than the first.

> He loves seeing His grace exalted and watching it change us into His image.

When we respond to our Father's discipline by humbling ourselves with the "godly sorrow" of true repentance (2 Cor. 7:11), He will pour out His mercy on us. It's never too late, and you are never too far gone, to receive the restoring power of the One who loves you.

Let all who take refuge in You be glad,
let them ever sing for joy; and may You shelter them,
that those who love Your name may exult in You.
PSALM 5:11

— He Speaks to Me —

Is there any area of your life that you feel is "too far gone" for God's mercy to save you? Offer it to Him in prayer today, and receive His forgiveness and grace to move forward.

If we confess our sins, He is faithful and righteous to forgive us our sins and to cleanse us from all unrighteousness.
1 John 1:9

For God did not send the Son into the world to judge the world, but that the world might be saved through Him.
JOHN 3:17

Recycled Parts

―――――――――― ❀ ――――――――――

Do not go on presenting the members of your body
to sin as instruments of unrighteousness; but present
yourselves to God as those alive from the dead.
ROMANS 6:13

G rowing up, I received more discipline from my parents than all three of my other siblings combined. I recall more than once coming home with a letter from my teacher explaining why I'd been sent to the principal's office. My parents would typically take me back to a bedroom down the hall from where all the other bedrooms were located, where we would, um . . . talk about it. (Ahem.)

If there was a theme to my troublemaking, it generally involved something to do with "that mouth," as my mother sometimes called it. "That mouth," from all disciplinary indications, seemed destined to cause me a lifetime of trouble if I didn't get it under control.

Or at least take it in a different direction.

My parents were patient and discerning. They were the first to see the potential in this "problem." They planted the idea in my head that my aptitude for talking could actually be a benefit to me, even to others. They encouraged me to read to our family some of the poetry and monologues I'd been writing. And over time, through opportunities like teaching a children's Sunday school class, giving presentations behind the microphone at church, and studying communications as a college student, God repurposed a potential negative into something that actually had a useful place in His kingdom. I suppose He knew what He was doing all along when He created me with this talkative temperament.

And I'm not the first to discover this transformation.

When Saul from Tarsus was surprised with a sudden lightning flash along a roadside and transformed into the most prolific Christian missionary of all time, it was not by chance. God chose a man "of the nation of Israel, of the tribe of Benjamin, a Hebrew of Hebrews; as to the Law, a Pharisee; as to zeal, a persecutor of the church" (Phil. 3:5–6), someone whose past ideally prepared him to understand what God's Word had been saying about Jesus all these years, and who understood the power of the church so keenly that he'd done everything he could do to stamp it out.

The selection of Paul as His most out-front ambassador to the first-century world was not an accident. Those qualities that had turned him so ferociously against the Way would become the same powder keg that God would light on fire in championing the gospel against savage opposition. Paul would need every ounce of that tenacity to fulfill his purpose. The tools that made him dangerous became the trademarks of his destiny.

> The tools that made him dangerous became the trademarks of his destiny.

This is God's way—turning negatives into positives. Reshaping and molding temperaments and propensities by His Spirit till they are suitable for kingdom purpose. Start seeing your child or spouse or friend through that light. Then see *yourself* through that lens as well. The parts that get you into the most trouble, if recycled for God's glory, might just turn a world upside down.

You—all of who *you* are—is capable of achieving some astounding and God-glorifying triumphs. Submit it all to Him—the good and the bad—and watch Him use it in ways you could have never imagined.

I will restore to you the years that the swarming locust has eaten.
JOEL 2:25 ESV

— He Speaks to Me —

What are some of the weaknesses, in yourself or someone you love, that you've discounted as possible tools that God can use for His glory? How can you see Him transforming them into truly effective strengths?

Those members of the body which we deem less honorable, on these we bestow more abundant honor, and our less presentable members become much more presentable.
1 Corinthians 12:23

*The scorched land will become a pool and
the thirsty ground springs of water.*
Isaiah 35:7

Baby Steps

🐝

She did what she could.
MARK 14:8 NIV

My year-old niece wobbled on unsteady legs, headed toward the cool, blue waters of the swimming pool nearly fifteen feet away. Her father and older siblings were already immersed inside, calling for her to join them. But she was still fairly new at this walking business. It didn't come as effortlessly to her as to those who'd been doing it a while. Her tempo was erratic and uneven. It lacked the smooth cadence that can only be gained by experience. Even something so simple required, for her, careful calculation.

I watched from a comfortable, silent distance, taking in the sweet scene. At one point, arms flailing, I felt sure she'd be toppling to the pavement any second, a precursor of the wailing cry that was sure to flare up from her scraped knee through her offended lungs. But instead of folding to fear or caving to comparisons . . .

She did what she could.

Jesus was never one to demean or minimize people's well-intentioned, pure-hearted efforts, no matter how meager or paltry. When a marginalized widow brought only a couple of measly coins to drop gingerly into the collection box, He praised her as a rich example to follow. All the others who were flinging their surplus currency into the same offering container would do well to learn a lesson from her. She did what she could, this unnamed widow who still inspires us with her sacrifice. Doing all she could do was enough.

In many seasons of life, we're prone to wonder if our wobbly, unsteady steps in any one direction are actually worth the painstaking effort they require. We're tempted to just withhold our offering—whether of time, talents, or treasure—assuming it will never be ample enough to interest the Lord's attention, figuring that others would label it a complete waste. We question whether small steps, uneven steps, unsteady steps, can ever be worthy steps—worthy enough to please Him, strong enough to propel us toward our destiny.

And yet Jesus doesn't point out our lack or magnify our deficiency. He doesn't consult the opinions of others to determine the significance of our efforts. Our kind, tender, humble Lord is more likely to look us squarely in the eyes and whisper words like these, words that should lift the unwarranted pressure from our weary shoulders . . .

Beloved, do what you can.

Take that step. Offer that service. Submit that idea. Set that goal. Say that prayer. Make that request. Use those talents. Do what you can. What *you* can.

Don't do nothing just because you can't do everything.

Don't do nothing just because you can't do everything. Don't hang back in safe complacency, sure that no gift of yours would matter anyway. Move forward—flailing arms and all—knowing that fledgling, unsteady strides become strong, secure ones over time. Today's steps are building the strong foundation for tomorrow's successes.

"Who has despised the day of small things?" (Zech. 4:10). Not us.

Not anymore. We're moving forward. One step at a time.

He who is faithful in a very little thing is faithful also in much.
LUKE 16:10

— He Speaks to Me —

What are one or two of those small steps the Spirit of God has been compelling you to take lately? Take them. Today.

He will bless those who fear the Lord,
the small together with the great.
Psalm 115:13

Though your beginning was insignificant,
yet your end will increase greatly.
JOB 8:7

No Offense

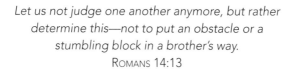

Let us not judge one another anymore, but rather determine this—not to put an obstacle or a stumbling block in a brother's way.
ROMANS 14:13

The Devil had his chance to pile on judgment against us for all our sin. We gave him plenty of ammunition to launch, given our bent toward unrighteousness and our antagonism to God's ways. But our kind Father "made Him who knew no sin to be sin on our behalf, so that we might become the righteousness of God in Him" (2 Cor. 5:21). "There is now no condemnation for those who are in Christ Jesus" (Rom. 8:1).

Hallelujah, there's nothing left to judge here.

And since the Enemy can't judge us, he wants to turn us into judges.

In any gathering of people in Jesus' name, in any collection of the redeemed where a local church comes together, the opportunity exists for being critical, thinking the worst, holding grudges, and taking offense.

And our Enemy loves this. *Togetherness* is one of the main things he wants to assault. He wants us isolated. He wants us on our own. He doesn't want us to recognize the power of being part of a body, part of the family of God. He wants us embittered, laden with unforgiveness, pointing fingers, and separated by suspicions of betrayal. So he pokes and prods us toward judgment of those around us until, even as we stand beneath the free-flowing shower of our Father's grace, we aren't willing to release that same grace to our brothers and sisters.

In the passage best known for its description of the armor of God (Ephesians 6), one of the items listed is the "shield of faith" (v. 16). The function of this piece of spiritual protection, Paul said, is to help us "be able to extinguish all the flaming arrows of the evil one." Among the common tactics in ancient Roman warfare was the practice of shooting these "fiery darts," as the King James puts it. The purpose of launching them, however, was not so much to kill as to create distraction. The entry of flaming arrows into the opposing camp would set the supplies on fire and threaten their living quarters. The enemy knew, if they could force the fighting men to break ranks in order to tend to these haphazard blazes, they could exploit the resulting holes and weaknesses in the line. Those little flashes of trouble that needed putting out would keep the army too busy to fight back or hold their ground.

Togetherness is one of the main things he wants to assault.

When we break ranks with our fellow "soldiers" through our little side squabbles and quarrels, we take the church off mission and off vision— precisely what the Enemy wants. The line of defense against him is weakened and he can infiltrate more easily. We can't let him keep tricking us that way. We must stay united, committed to each other, defending each other, rather than creating separation that only exposes us all to more attack.

"Let us not judge one another anymore," because we're only playing into his hand when we do. By standing together, not even the gates of hell can stand against us.

There is only one Lawgiver and Judge, the One who is able to save and to destroy; but who are you who judge your neighbor?
JAMES 4:12

— He Speaks to Me —

Who is the person(s) you tend to judge the most? What advantage do you think the Enemy will gain by this division? Ask the Lord to give you sensitivity to others and insight on how to "close ranks."

*Accept one another, just as Christ also
accepted us to the glory of God.*
ROMANS 15:7

If you bite and devour one another, watch out,
or you will be consumed by one another.
GALATIANS 5:15 CSB

Who Stole My Rhino?

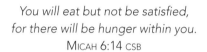

You will eat but not be satisfied,
for there will be hunger within you.
Micah 6:14 csb

Friends of ours were blessed to go on an African safari as a family. The jeeps rolled through tall grass and over bumpy terrain, carrying people dressed in their loose-fitting, savanna-colored clothes, binoculars poised and ready for the next observation stop.

The understood goal of most safaris is being able to check off the sighting of the "Big Five" from the list of animals spotted with your own eyes in the wild. These include a particular species of (1) elephant, (2) rhinoceros, (3) buffalo, (4) lion, and (5) leopard. Fill your card with confirmed sightings of all five, and people will say you've lived the safari dream.

But like anything, some safaris are a success and some aren't. Eyeballing each of these five target animals isn't guaranteed, only hoped for. In our friends' case, they'd been fortunate enough to see four of them, with one more day remaining in which to hopefully add the fifth. But try as they might, the fifth species eluded them.

I'm told that one of the family members fretted through the whole last day, missing the opportunity to appreciate many of the highlights that the others were enjoying because he was so obsessed over that last missing animal on his Big Five list. In *his* mind, if he couldn't call in the rhino, he couldn't call it a good day. His attitude was sullen, his perspective grim, the beautiful experience dampened.

This is what discontentment always does. It dampens our delight in things we already have and to the bounty that currently surrounds us. It blinds us to the "Big Four"—which, frankly, are really astounding already and should compel us to gratitude, not be overlooked as not quite enough.

What's the one thing that's making your *Big Five* an unsatisfying *Big Four?* What's the one thing—*the one thing*—that is eluding your grasp and consuming your attention, diverting it away from the abundance and blessing all around you? The *one thing* you can't have or can't do? The *one thing* you want but haven't seen happening yet in your marriage or family or finances or career or ministry?

> Contentment comes from valuing what you've been given, not venting over what's been withheld.

Don't let it overshadow all the beautiful, bountiful things you could be enjoying and celebrating and soaking up today. Refuse to allow those missing elements to keep you from fully engaging in what's around you. Contentment comes from valuing what you've been given, not venting over what's been withheld.

In hindsight, our friend looks back and realizes how he missed an opportunity to truly engage and enjoy the full safari experience with his family. He recognizes that his lack of gratitude for the *Big Four* cost him a hefty price he no longer wants to pay in his life. He wants what we all should—to wring every last drop of goodness out of the life we *do* have, the life that's already sprawling out before us.

The apostle Paul expressed this principle beautifully when he said, "I have learned to be content whatever the circumstances" (Phil. 4:11 NIV). And if there's *one thing* you learn today, let this one truth be it.

Who of you by being worried can add a single hour to his life?
MATTHEW 6:27

— He Speaks to Me —

Write down your "Big Four"—the things God has already given, but things you've discounted because of something else that's still missing. Celebrate His here-and-now blessings today.

The boundary lines have fallen for me in pleasant places;
indeed, I have a beautiful inheritance.
PSALM 16:6 CSB

As for me, I shall behold Your face in righteousness;
I will be satisfied with Your likeness when I awake.

Of Trees and Integrity

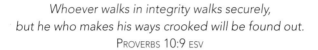

Whoever walks in integrity walks securely,
but he who makes his ways crooked will be found out.
<small>PROVERBS 10:9 ESV</small>

It was the kind of storm that makes you snuggle down deeper into your bedcovers—rain peppering the rooftop, lightning strobes illuminating the windowpanes. But it wasn't so nice the next morning when we looked out and saw that it had claimed one of our tallest, most majestic trees, crashing it to the ground in the backyard.

When we ventured outside to inspect the damage, we were shocked at what we saw. This huge, towering tree that had always stood so strong, straight, and dignified had snapped in two like a flimsy twig. And inside the fractured trunk, now painfully exposed, lay a husk of splintered, rotten, decaying wood. We couldn't believe a tree that looked so healthy and stable from all outward appearance could be so moldy and compromised underneath.

Such deterioration hadn't happened overnight, the tree expert told us when he came to haul off the remains the next day. This kind of decay had undoubtedly been steeping for months—starting small but ruining the structure and strength of the whole tree over time. For years it had looked sturdy on the outside while it was rotting away on the inside.

It didn't have . . . *integrity.*

Downed trees are like toppled lives: a veneer of strength disguising a steady, internal decline, happening somewhere beneath the skin we allow others to see. People think we're fine, perhaps even exemplary. They're drawn to the image we create, the same as my family and I were drawn to this piece of property by its cove of tall, gorgeous trees. I could already imagine them towering over my boys on their routine afternoons of play.

But whenever our character lacks symmetry with our external appearance, when piety is only painted on for effect, we will sooner or later implode. Our lives eventually won't be able to support their own weight, nor provide the shade and blessing we desire for our families and others. "Be sure your sin will find you out," the Bible famously says (Num. 32:23). We can't keep hypocrisy hidden forever. We're either structurally sound or we're structurally compromised.

We can't keep hypocrisy hidden forever.

We need to avoid this messy fallout altogether, to choose longevity over license. Rather than hoping nobody ever sees, rather than hoping our old roots will surely be enough to keep us standing upright (like always before), it's time to spare ourselves the exhaustion and just line up our inside with our outside. *Alignment* is the answer. The freedom and beauty of integrity will do more good for our hearts than whatever seems so much more desirable in the short term.

Ask the Lord for courage to create a balance between the unseen portions of your life and the parts that others observe. Invite Him to scoop out the deadwood through confession and repentance, and let Him create fresh growth in your weakened places.

Then you'll be steady. Strong. Built to last.

If you possess these qualities in increasing measure,
they will keep you from being ineffective and unproductive
in your knowledge of our Lord Jesus Christ.
2 PETER 1:8 NIV

— He Speaks to Me —

Where do you hope to be standing in the next five to ten years? Can you do it with what's living beneath the surface? Does it match what everybody sees?

I will give them one heart and one way, that they may fear Me always, for their own good and for the good of their children after them.
JEREMIAH 32:39

Teach me Your way, O LORD; I will walk in Your truth; unite my heart to fear Your name.
PSALM 86:11

Hearing Is Believing

Behold, the champion, the Philistine of Gath,
Goliath by name, came up out of the ranks of the Philistines
and spoke the same words as before. And David heard him.
1 Samuel 17:23 esv

*D*avid and Goliath. This story and the themes it represents are so thoroughly familiar, tempting us to skim the passage and hurry through instead of mining the treasures beneath the surface. But since the layers of meaning in God's Word are truly boundless and are ready to be accentuated by the Spirit's voice, He will always make good on His promise to open up His Word to us in a refreshing and (dare I say) *new* kind of way.

The Philistine giant stood nine-feet, nine-inches tall, imposing enough to cause even a hardened opposing soldier to quake in his boots. Taking one look at this enormous warrior, the Israelite army "fled from him and were greatly afraid" (1 Sam. 17:24). But notice a little phrase that's sometimes lost in all the battleground noise and slingshot action. Israel *watched*; David *listened*.

"David *heard* him."

Whereas the soldiers' perspective was shaped solely by what they *saw* in this massive force of brute fighting stature, David's perspective was formed by what he *heard*—Goliath mocking the armies and power of the living God. And that's what made the difference. If he'd only been going by what he could see, he might have felt like shrinking back with all the rest of them. But as soon as he "heard" what was coming from Goliath's mouth, he was unafraid to advance against even a fearsome enemy.

Likely you are currently dealing with one or more problems or battles in life that are of Goliath-sized proportions—big and looming, perhaps to the point of becoming dire and desperate. But visual impressions only yield part of the story. What are you *hearing* from the midst of them? Are you hearing how impotent your God is to do anything about it? Are you hearing insinuations that contradict His Word and His good, Fatherly intentions toward you? Are you hearing claims that your plight is hopeless, that this is the end for you, that your faith in persevering is nothing but a big waste of time?

> Visual impressions only yield part of the story.

Remember David's example. Don't allow the frightening names, dates, and specifics of your situation to send you cowering. Let the lies and falsehood stir a holy indignation that rises up in your soul. Galvanize yourself in God's Spirit with a courageous responsibility for standing tall on His Word and strong in His truth, because nothing can thwart God's purposes, even amid the most vicious challenges you face. Rise up with His counsel from Scripture, indignant against every lie you're hearing, then head out into battle to slay that giant in Jesus' name.

He awakens my ear to listen like those being instructed. The Lord God has opened my ear, and I was not rebellious; I did not turn back.
Isaiah 50:4–5 csb

— He Speaks to Me —

What types of things are your fiercest battles "saying" to you right now? Be proactive in locating and claiming the truth of God to quell them.

_____

_____

_____

_____

_____

_____

_____

_____

_____

_____

_____

_____

At whatever place you hear the sound of the trumpet,
rally to us there. Our God will fight for us.
NEHEMIAH 4:20

*Those that were sown on the good soil are
the ones who hear the word and accept it and bear fruit.*
MARK 4:20 ESV

Worth the Wait

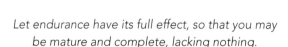

*Let endurance have its full effect, so that you may
be mature and complete, lacking nothing.*
JAMES 1:4 CSB

Baking homemade bread is much more difficult than it appears. I had watched a friend work her magic with yeast, dough roller, and oven, and had tasted the glorious results she produced. So I decided to try my hand at it too—not realizing it would be a year and a half before I could pull out any soft, billowing, golden loaves to match hers. Yes, nearly two years of perfecting it. Some were nice tries, but others were pretty sad. My family chomped their way through quite a few dense, heavy batches that were advertised with seductive aroma from the kitchen but fell a little flat in the execution.

Honestly, it was a frustrating process, requiring a great deal of time, patience, diligence, and detail.

But some dreams, I've found, are like that. They take months and years before they finally come to fruition. In fact, the more worthwhile and satisfying they are, the longer they generally take to accomplish. Like the walls of Jerusalem that took Nehemiah fifty-two days to rebuild. Like Solomon's Temple, which took seven years to construct. Like the Israelites' forty-year trek through the wilderness of Sinai to the Promised Land—their hearts being refined in the heat of the desert. Some things— things worth having and achieving—take time to complete.

Readings in those early books of the Old Testament can often seem tedious and fraught with endless minutiae. We are often tempted to skip some of the more detailed stories and circumstances. But in those pages we see that God was working on *people,* not just the *projects* that those people were trying to complete. And the transformation of those people took time. He was revealing His nature to them, introducing them to principles of obedience and blessing, and of sin and repercussions. But in the struggle for them to understand—even in our struggle to hang in there when we read their stories—He leads us to Jesus. It was all meant to take them (and us) to Jesus. The wait and the work are worth it. For all of us.

Is there a goal you've been working toward? An ambition or dream you've been aiming to reach? The Lord knows how many hours you've put in and how much energy you've expended. He's not unaware or ambivalent to your diligence. He knows your hardships and frustrations. And with every step, He's been working right along with you, nipping and tucking and turning you into a version of you that's becoming increasingly mature. Complete. Lacking nothing. This kind of work—this masterpiece—doesn't happen overnight. It takes time.

> God was working on *people,* not just the *projects* that those people were trying to complete.

So keep pressing into it, breaking it down into smaller-sized portions that don't appear quite so overwhelming. Endure. The day is coming—sooner than you think—when you'll not only be able to enjoy the fruit of your diligence, but you'll see that while you were working on *it,* God was working on *you.*

And that'll taste pretty sweet.

May you be strengthened with all power, according to his glorious might, for all endurance and patience with joy.
COLOSSIANS 1:11 ESV

— He Speaks to Me —

What is some of the growth and development you can pinpoint in your own life recently?

_To those who by patience in well-doing seek for
glory and honor and immortality, he will give eternal life._
ROMANS 2:7 ESV

Moses persevered as one who sees him who is invisible.
HEBREWS 11:27 CSB

— Day 42 —

The Late Shift

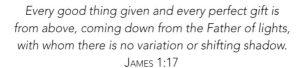

*Every good thing given and every perfect gift is
from above, coming down from the Father of lights,
with whom there is no variation or shifting shadow.*
JAMES 1:17

Every year that passes delivers a real, tangible reminder of
the effects of time. Hard, sculpted bodies soften. Smooth,
youthful faces wrinkle. Slender, narrow feet swell or flatten. Taut, firm skin loosens and fails to cooperate. Every week
the mirror introduces us to a person we don't entirely recognize.
Whenever we find a picture of us, taken from two, three, four
years ago or more—my goodness, we'd almost forgotten. Did we
really wear our hair that way? Did we really fit into that top? Did
we really have such smooth skin?

Time reveals the temporal. It highlights the slow but steady
decline that everyone on Earth is subject to experiencing.
Everything changes. Nothing stays the same—not the way we
once knew it. Jobs become deleted. Prices go up. Children take
on new interests and grow into different paths. Particular foods
we once enjoyed without a second thought now keep us up at
night with heartburn. The workout that always sufficed doesn't
budge the scales like it once did. Maintaining our energy level is
not the effortless task it used to be. Things we'd counted on to be
there when we reached a certain age fail to come together as we'd
planned, even as certain people we admired prove unfaithful and
fractured.

Life just refuses to stay put.

And yet God stays the same.

His Word, His truth, Himself.

Unchanged.

The older I get, the more I notice and love—and am frankly astonished at the power of—this quality in His nature. He shows up every single morning without any "variation or shifting shadow." Always the same. Ever constant. Unchanging. Unmoving. He is the first and the last. Eternity in our midst—His Spirit fresh and alive in us, same as on the day we first met Him—His mercies new with each approaching sunrise. "Your years," the psalmist said of Him, "will not come to an end" (Ps. 102:27). He will always *be* who He's always *been*, no matter how quickly time passes or how many changes we're forced to navigate.

Reminding yourself of this fact today should give you confidence—a confidence you will need in these ever-changing times. He will never cease being faithful and good, strong and true. He will always be light, with "absolutely no darkness in him" (1 John 1:5 csb). He will always be "love" (1 John 4:16), even on days when you feel the most condemned and unforgivable. The Son will always live "to make intercession" for you (Heb. 7:25), never leaving you exposed and alone and without "an Advocate with the Father" (1 John 2:1). You may feel tempted to worry or be concerned about a lot of new developments, but you never need to wonder whether or not you'll find God eternally trustworthy in the midst of them.

> He will always be who He's always been.

Each year may be new to *us*, but He is the same yesterday, today, and forever.

The Lord is good; His lovingkindness is everlasting
and His faithfulness to all generations.
PSALM 100:5

— He Speaks to Me —

How does a reminder of God's unchanging nature offer reassurance in the wake of any recent change in your circumstances?

He is the living God, and he endures forever; his kingdom will never be destroyed, and his dominion has no end.
DANIEL 6:26 CSB

Heaven and earth will pass away,
but My words will not pass away.
Matthew 24:35

Results May Vary

⚜

Other seed fell on good ground and produced fruit: some a
hundred, some sixty, and some thirty times what was sown.
MATTHEW 13:8 CSB

*I*t was an odd sight—two identical plants sitting side by side in
the same flower bed at my cousin's house. They'd been watered
by the same irrigation, nourished by the same nutrients from
the same exact soil. Yet one was green, lush, and vibrant, while
the other was brown, dry, and brittle.

Strange.

And yet maybe not quite so uncommon. Not in our Christian
life at least.

In Jesus' familiar parable of the sower, all of the seeds that
were planted on "good ground" or in "good soil" resulted in a
crop (Matt. 13:23). A *good* crop. All of them were considered
productive. But some were *less* productive than others. A thirty-
fold yield is naturally not as healthy as sixtyfold, nor is sixtyfold
as desirable as a hundredfold. Something kept the seed from
being as prodigious in one area of the field as another.

And this discrepancy, along with those two bushes I spotted
in that flower bed, got me to wondering: Why would that be? If
the soil is the same, why wouldn't the seed do the same thing in
one place as in another? Why wouldn't all the bushes blossom
equally?

Hundreds of believers can sit in the same church, sing the
same songs, be fed from the same Word, and share from the
same spiritual table. Yet the fruit that is produced in one person's
life from the implanted Word of God can vary widely from that
which is produced in another. One woman may handle a crisis

with resilient faith that grows stronger and more precious in the process, while another withers and grows more prickly to the touch. One man may become bold and effervescent in sharing the love of Christ with others, while another goes his whole life without ever mentioning the name of Jesus to anyone at work or in his neighborhood.

Same soil, different harvest.

That's because some believers are willing to do the hard work of appropriating and utilizing the spiritual nutrients being offered to them, while others sit back in apathetic indolence. Without proactive and intentional action, they find themselves lacking the fruit they admire in others.

Worse yet, they can become satisfied with their lackluster harvest and lazily idle themselves in others' shade. But close proximity with people who are bearing hundred-fold returns does not guarantee the same rate of return in ourselves. The soil can be the same, and yet the harvest completely different.

> The soil can be the same, and yet the harvest completely different.

Each of us must individually do the work of tending to the seed that's been planted—renewing our minds, yielding to His Spirit, devoting ourselves to prayer, and living with a God-centered perspective.

Don't settle for less than all He wants to produce through your life. Resist the urge to sit by and let other people's spiritual vibrancy substitute for yours. Grow and keep on growing until God gets the absolute most from what He's specifically planted in you. Tend your soil. Take care of your seed. Yield a fruitful harvest.

Bear fruit in keeping with repentance.
MATTHEW 3:8

— He Speaks to Me —

Is there any way in which you've settled for less of a harvest than you think God intends?

It was planted in good soil beside abundant waters, that it might yield branches and bear fruit and become a splendid vine.
EZEKIEL 17:8

173

You are God's field, God's building.
1 Corinthians 3:9

Whole Wide World

*This gospel of the kingdom shall be preached
in the whole world as a testimony to all the nations.*
MATTHEW 24:14

I attended a tea function in a Pacific Rim city one morning,
part of a conference that had brought together more than
fourteen thousand women from nearly forty different coun-
tries and two dozen denominations. From my standpoint at that
event, the visible proof of God's global work was everywhere
I turned. Eastern Europeans conversing with people from the
American Midwest. Women from London being introduced to
Christian leaders from Asia. Ladies with expressive Hispanic
accents laughing and sharing stories with others who spoke the
common love language of Christ's family.

The kaleidoscope of God's body was represented there. And
even though it was still only a miniature version, it was enough
to blow my mind, to recalibrate my ethnocentric, geocentric
compass readings. It made me not want to filter out the vast
scope of His mission or keep it funneled so tightly around my
own city and nation and mailing address.

Right this moment—in Peru, Australia, South Africa,
Ukraine, New Zealand, Uganda, and countless places around
the globe—the whole wide world of God's kingdom is up and
moving. His people on every continent are serving Him and
needing Him and loving Him and leading others to love Him,
just like you and your church are doing in your own particular
corner of the world. Our incredible family of brothers and sisters
are living and working, praying and trusting, watching Him do

in their local context the same kind of activity and transformation that we love seeing Him do in ours.

And it's really easy to forget this. To forget how big His operation is. To forget how infinitesimally small our own full plate is. To forget the enormity of His purposes, happening all the time amid the many colors and languages and denominational styles of His many, many children. We forget that He is always moving everywhere, in ways beyond our imagination—and that if we would truly open our eyes and ears to the Spirit's prompting, He could show us all-new opportunities for grasping His global vision in our minds and investing our prayer and passion into it more fully than ever.

We forget that He is always moving everywhere.

If you and I spend all of our weeks just going to *our* church, going about *our* business, and worrying about *our* tomorrows, we'll miss out on the huge work God is doing in *our* world. Lift your eyes from the narrow circle of your own life to the broad beauty of God's activity and opportunity being done this morning through his church all over the world. It is certainly a sight to behold.

I looked, and behold, a great multitude which no one could count, from every nation and all tribes and peoples and tongues, standing before the throne and before the Lamb.
REVELATION 7:9

— He Speaks to Me —

Ask God to show you even one place where you could begin directing your prayer beyond your borders.

The earth will be filled with the knowledge of the glory of the LORD, as the waters cover the sea.
HABAKKUK 2:14

Forgiveness of sins would be proclaimed in
His name to all the nations.
Luke 24:47

Home Alone

✦

*The torrent burst against that house and could
not shake it, because it had been well built.*
LUKE 6:48

A neighborhood of two hundred homes near Galveston, Texas, took a direct hit from a monstrous hurricane, roaring in from the Gulf of Mexico. Every single house was completely destroyed, flattened to nothing but bricks, sticks, and foundation slicks.

All except one. *One.*

And this one was not only still standing but was seemingly untouched. The window frames, the porch railings, the gables, the chimney—all of it was there, as if the storm had picked up its feet for a split second in advance of that particular home on the building plat and then pounded them right back down to the ground again the moment it reached the other side.

The story in the newspaper was riveting. The images, unbelievable. In trying to determine an explanation for the house's survival (other than God's own sovereign hand), an interview with the homeowner revealed a specific, possible reason. And whether it's what saved this particular home or not, it definitely has something to say about our own success at surviving the unexpected storms of life.

This house had been mangled three years earlier by *another* hurricane. And the owners had made the expensive, extensive decision to rebuild, utilizing the skill of a master builder who specialized in designing structures sturdy enough to withstand the kinds of storms accustomed to hitting that area. When the hurricane howled this time, the craftsmanship they'd employed in strengthening their home at its core made it more impenetrable than others around it. If they'd opted for cheaper fixes, if they'd taken their chances that lightning would never strike twice in the same place—and especially if all they'd done was *talk* about rebuilding but never put their plan into *action*—their home would probably have been like the others, scattered across miles of depressing debris.

The way we build—it matters. The quality of materials we utilize to construct our lives matters. Isn't that what Jesus said when He asked, "Why do you call Me, 'Lord, Lord,' and do not do what I say? Everyone who comes to Me and hears My words and acts on them, I will show you whom he is like: he is like a man building a house, who dug deep and laid a foundation on the rock; and when a flood occurred, the torrent burst against that house and could not shake it, because it had been well built" (Luke 6:46–49).

The strength of being "on the rock."

"That house . . . could not shake."

"It had been well built."

> Your choice of building material determines your future.

Your choice of building material determines your future. Digging deep, hitting bedrock, and pouring a solid foundation on Christ alone and His Word alone are what secures you solidly to the ground. Because, listen to me, the storms are coming. And yet you can be strong, steeled, and storm-proofed because you've not only *heard* what the Spirit says, but you've put hammer to nail and implemented it into your architecture.

Be wise. Build well. Recommit yourself today to constructing the kind of life that Jesus said would withstand the stiffest gales of difficulty.

Every house is built by someone,
but the builder of all things is God.
HEBREWS 3:4

— He Speaks to Me —

Where are some of the leaks and weak spots in the structure of your life? What is God asking you to implement that will begin to fix and fortify them?

He will be the stability of your times,
a wealth of salvation, wisdom and knowledge.
Isaiah 33:6

Unless the LORD builds the house,
they labor in vain who build it.
PSALM 127:1

Little Captive Girl

❧

*She said to her mistress, "I wish that my master
were with the prophet who is in Samaria!
Then he would cure him of his leprosy."*
2 KINGS 5:3

Your Father's sovereignty is so complete, His dominion so comprehensive, and His control over even your most difficult circumstances so sure, there's really no situation in your life that is beyond His redeeming power. Not. Even. One.

Somehow, even your most grim dilemmas contain the essential ingredients from which He can extract peace and hope and—yes, even a good, remarkable ending.

Take the case of a little nameless, faceless girl thrust onto the landscape of Scripture as a political captive. A native of Israel, she had been taken during a raid on her homeland and forced into slavery, ending up in the service of an army captain's wife. It was hardly the outcome she could have wanted, yanked away from the familiar, pressed into the dangerous unfamiliar. Yet in a twist of logic that's hard for the frail, human mind to grasp, the Bible says *God* was the one who'd been behind this conquering of His people. "The LORD had given victory to Aram" (2 Kings 5:1). His sovereignty had been actively involved in this dire situation.

And believe it or not, His sovereignty is involved in yours too. Everything that happens to you is either *ordained* by God or *allowed* by God. Even the outworking of evil that touches your life must first pass through His loving fingers before it intersects with you. Somehow, He funnels it all toward a glorious outcome for your good in which His name is made great and His purposes are served. That's why this little girl, while a captive in Syria, found herself in the ironically ideal spot for exalting her God in a strange land.

Her master, Naaman, was a leper. And in the course of this girl's work for Naaman's wife, she was brave enough to declare that the power of God could heal him. Yet not only did her faith and courage eventually lead this pagan soldier to testify, "I know that there is no God in all the earth, but in Israel" (v. 15), but even Jesus, centuries later, in testifying of Himself as Messiah, pointed back to this healing of Naaman—sparked into action by a little captive girl—as proof of His radical love and ministry to the Gentiles. Her story was still speaking volumes. And continues speaking them still.

> God has a sovereign plan, and you are a part of it.

So today, if your current circumstances are not what you ever imagined they'd be—if your dreams have been dashed and your expectations unmet—if you've been taken captive by life, as if kidnapped into an unfamiliar reality that you'd rather escape—and if you can't understand why anything like this should be happening to you—remember, God has a sovereign plan, and you are a part of it.

This little girl could not have known the significance of her capture in the grand design of Yahweh's sovereign agenda. And neither can you. But if you'll trust Him, accepting what you can't understand, you'll see He has only diverted you onto the center stage of His will.

We know that God causes all things to work together for good to those who love God, to those who are called according to His purpose.
Romans 8:28

— He Speaks to Me —

Thank the Lord for His sovereignty over every circumstance in your life. Ask Him to renew your confidence that He can use your current position for His purposes and your good.

I know that You can do all things, and that
no purpose of Yours can be thwarted.
JOB 42:2

You meant evil against me, but God meant it for good in order to bring about this present result, to preserve many people alive.
GENESIS 50:20

Overshadowed

Mary said to the angel, "How can this be, since I am a virgin?"
The angel answered and said to her, "The Holy Spirit will come
upon you, and the power of the Most High will overshadow you."
LUKE 1:34–35

Something special and unique accompanies any authentic work of God. Activities initiated by the Holy Spirit have outcomes that transcend those that originate with *us*, in *our* minds, through *our* effort. While He may graciously allow us to actively participate in His work—which is a miracle in itself—the aftermaths and results of it will clearly be beyond explanation. This is the nature of the supernatural. They defy normal appraisals of opinion or expectation. Instead, by some measure, they are beyond belief.

Because they are born of the Holy Spirit.

Take the birth of Jesus as the ultimate example.

Jesus' arrival on planet Earth is set apart as the most supernatural experience of all time. It hangs in the balance of history as the great dividing line between *before* and *after*—the hinge upon which His plan of redemption rests. Obviously then, this kind of miraculous occurrence could not be left up to human planning, organization, strategizing, and industry. Its genesis couldn't afford to be blemished and marred by mortal fingerprints. It needed the Holy Spirit's moving, producing, creating, overshadowing. It needed to be sparked in such a way that no one could possibly explain such an unexplainable act except by crediting it to divine intervention. All human factors had to be swallowed up by the holy, leading to the kind of amazement that would leave young Mary breathless, saying . . .

"How? How can this be?"

And while the Son's incarnate entrance into our world was truly a one-of-a-kind, unrepeatable event, the Spirit wasn't finished amazing us with His handiwork. He still intends to excite this same sort of stunned, staggered reaction from your soul (and from the souls of those around you) by accomplishing things through you that only He can do. He wants to produce things through your life that would have been impossible without Him. Then while others may applaud you, congratulate you, and put their compliments into kind words to offer you, you'll know deep down that these accolades don't really belong to you. You'll know Who really did the work, and You'll know to deflect all glory back to Him. You'll look into the heavens, thinking, *How can this be? How did You do that?*

You'll know for sure it wasn't *you.*

You'll know Who really did the work.

Desire this. Ask God for this. Resist the urge to shy away or shrink back from those things that only God's Spirit can accomplish, and then resist the urge to take credit for it when it's done. God intends to birth in you dreams and potential that will be marked by the Holy Spirit. They will stretch you beyond your own natural limitations and will be a spectacular display of His power at work in your life. Step humbly into His light, and rejoice in the beauty of being overshadowed.

"Not by might nor by power,
but by My Spirit," says the LORD of hosts.
ZECHARIAH 4:6

— He Speaks to Me —

How might you be sensing God calling you out beyond yourself, into something only He can do?

Some boast in chariots and some in horses,
but we will boast in the name of the Lord, our God.
PSALM 20:7

The Spirit is the one who gives life. The flesh doesn't help at all.
The words that I have spoken to you are spirit and are life.
JOHN 6:63 *CSB*

Unbelievable Unity

_____ ✤ _____

He Himself is our peace, who made both groups
into one and broke down the barrier of the dividing wall.
EPHESIANS 2:14

Before the book of Ephesians became a beloved portion of the New Testament, it was a piece of smudged parchment circulating through the wealthy, commercial city of Ephesus in ancient Greece. The believers there would read it or would hear it read, then they would pass it along to others, perhaps even to other churches in neighboring cities.

And at each reading, these first-century Christians realized they were being asked to do something, to believe something, to support something that everyone knew was impossible— utterly, totally impossible. The writer of this letter, Paul the apostle, said that Jews and Gentiles—age-old enemies in every conceivable aspect of the word—were no longer to consider themselves as existing on opposite cultural planets. By virtue of the gospel, the two of them had now become a "mystery" race (Eph. 3:3–4) known as the body of Christ, a unity of believers designed to show the world that if God could do *this*, if He could bridge this cultural breach, He most certainly could do anything.

The idea of Jews and Gentiles getting along, respecting each other, cooperating together—no one had ever talked this way before. No one could see this happening. The fissures ran too deep. The haughtiness and hostility were too ingrained. They hated the ground the other walked on. Their aims and desires were mutually exclusive. By a country mile.

Yet as impossible as it sounded for this long-standing feud to finally end in a truce, Paul declared this their new reality. God had already done it. Beyond merely wishing these sworn rivals could sit down and figure out a way to play nice together, God just went ahead and "tore down the dividing wall of hostility" between them (Eph. 2:14 CSB)—the one that had stood there for dozens and dozens of long, gray-haired generations. He wasn't *appealing* for peace; He was *proclaiming* peace—"peace to you who were far away, and peace to those who were near" (Eph. 2:17). Through the life and death of His Son Jesus, it was done.

Jesus changed everything.

He *still* changes everything.

Wherever people are estranged and distant, unity in Jesus can bring them back into fellowship. Wherever families are broken and splintered apart, humble surrender to Jesus can begin putting things back together. Wherever the rift seems too wide and too complicated to repair, Jesus has already done what needs doing to fix it.

Now it's time for us to believe it. And go live like it.

The only thing left for the early church to do, once they'd heard this news, was to begin accepting by faith that what God had already accomplished, they could actually apply—not because of *their* power but because of *His*. And if God was able to do that—the ultimate impossibility in most of their minds—would anything else remain that He couldn't do? For them?

Or for you?

No. Not then. Not now. Not ever.

Things that are impossible with people are possible with God.
LUKE 18:27

— He Speaks to Me —

Record the names of people or people groups who seem separated from each other by an impossible divide. Thank the Lord for the peace He's established, and ask Him to allow His children to experience it.

By one Spirit we were all baptized into one body,
whether Jews or Greeks, whether slaves or free,
and we were all made to drink of one Spirit.
1 CORINTHIANS 12:13

Let the peace of Christ rule in your hearts,
to which indeed you were called in one body; and be thankful.
Colossians 3:15

One Thing at a Time

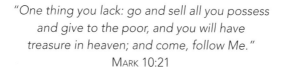

*"One thing you lack: go and sell all you possess
and give to the poor, and you will have
treasure in heaven; and come, follow Me."*
MARK 10:21

'll occasionally go to pull a necklace from the hook in my closet where I keep my long, spangled assortment of costume jewelry. And almost invariably, as I tug on the one I want, it will bring along with it three or four other necklaces, all tangled together into a stubborn knot.

My usual technique, in trying to separate them, is to grab where the knot seems to be the most entangled and start yanking at random strands, expecting to work everything free. Instead I only succeed at tightening the tangles and making everything worse. The secret, I've found, is to unhook the latch on *one* of the necklaces, and then trace that single cord out of the various places where it's become caught and twisted. Amazingly, by the time I get that *one* piece free, all the others have loosened up and become easier to untangle as well.

Focusing on *one thing* can lead to untangling *everything*.

A man came up to Jesus and, in the course of conversation, claimed his own exceptionality, describing how he'd accomplished all of the commandments that Jesus mentioned as being important ones to follow. Not only did he deem himself current on all his checkmarks, but "I have kept all these things from my youth up," he said (Mark 10:20). Imagine how full his days must have been, being perfect like that.

The Bible says, "Looking at him, Jesus loved him" (Mark 10:21 CSB). Imagine the tenderness, understanding, and redemption reflected in His eyes, giving to this pious man—who was tangled up in more sin, rebellion, and pride than he realized—something he didn't even think he needed. Jesus said to him, "One thing you lack."

In this case, the "one thing" Jesus brought to the man's mind was his attachment to money, to his stuff, to his wealth. "Go and sell all you possess and give to the poor." One thing. *Work on that one thing,* Jesus seemed to be saying. If he'd deal appropriately with that one thread, he'd start to see other snarled, tangled messes and questions of life begin to loosen. Obedience in this one thing would incite growth and freedom in other areas, as well as the opportunity to realize that what he truly needed for doing *anything* well was a relationship with the One who does *all* things well.

Sometimes it's just the one thing. If we'll only concentrate on doing the one thing . . .

> Focusing on *one thing* can lead to untangling everything.

When God's Spirit points out *one thing* that needs work in your life—perhaps a strand of pride or jealousy, a specific sin that needs refusing, a conversation you need to have, a relationship you need to lay down, an opportunity you need to engage—here's some advice. *Do that one thing.* Don't become overwhelmed by *everything.* Just obey in regard to the *one thing.* Concentrate on doing what God has most recently said, and see if it doesn't free up some of the other tangled messes of life that most concern you.

Please obey the Lord in what I am saying to you,
that it may go well with you and you may live.
JEREMIAH 38:20

— He Speaks to Me —

As you turn your attention to hear the Holy Spirit's leading, listen for the one thing—one place where He's pointing out your need for obedience. What is it? How do you plan to follow through on it?

The people said to Joshua, "We will serve
the Lord our God and we will obey His voice."
Joshua 24:24

I will always obey your instruction, forever and ever. I will walk freely in an open place because I study your precepts.
PSALM 119:44–45 CSB

Important Pieces

*"The King will answer and say to them, 'Truly I say to you,
to the extent that you did it to one of these brothers
of Mine, even the least of them, you did it to Me.'"*
MATTHEW 25:40

*I*was hungry," Jesus will say one day, sitting on His glorious throne, with all the people of all the nations gathered before Him. "I was hungry . . . I was thirsty . . . I was a stranger . . . naked . . . in prison . . ." (Matt. 25:35–36). And what did we do? With all those needs? With all that suffering? With all the examples of pain and loss, all over the world?

The coldness of heart and vaunted view of self that many have held will be sliced thin at Christ's words: "You gave Me nothing to eat . . . nothing to drink . . . did not invite Me in . . . did not clothe Me . . . did not visit Me" (vv. 42–43). It was *Him* all along, cloaked behind the veil of the marginalized and disenfranchised. We could have done something. *Anything.*

Take a look around you—at your home and the tasks to be done there, at your job and the assignments to be completed there, at your church and the service to be fulfilled there, in your community and the needs surfacing there. In each of these small circles, there is something a willing, compassionate heart must be willing to contribute. The Lord calls His children—bestowed with spiritual resources and lavished with His grace—beyond their own comfortable circle of blessing, into spaces where others' needs abound. He is calling you to open your heart more fully to Him so that you can minister with even greater compassion to those He brings to mind, out of your love and gratitude for what He's done for you.

No act of service is too small. The little piece you do matters. *Every piece matters.*

They're like ripples of water circling outward from a skipped rock. Everything you do creates an impact somewhere else you cannot see, but it's a part of the big picture that God is putting together. Your effort may not get written up in the newspaper. What you do might not guarantee the comprehensive end of poverty in your city or ensure that no one goes to bed cold on a wintry night. All of the crises will never fully be resolved in this cruel and fallen world. And yet it's our privilege, our joy, our mandate to extend Christ's love to others in a tangible, practical way.

Yes, God is moving everywhere—in homeless shelters and inner cities, among street children and AIDS patients, with unwed mothers and victims of sex trafficking. But one of those "everywheres" is the square footage where you and your local church live and care and help and minister, as well as in your prayer closet. Yours is a little piece of a big, masterful puzzle that connects together all these global efforts, and supernaturally connects each of us to each other in Jesus' mighty name.

> Everything you do creates an impact somewhere else you cannot see.

So do it. Give it. Extend it. Support it. Serve it. Care for it. Be a part of it. Whatever God has given you to do, do it with all of your heart and passion . . . because "even the least" is great when you do it for His sake.

Whoever receives this child in My name receives Me,
and whoever receives Me receives Him who sent Me.
LUKE 9:48

— He Speaks to Me —

Ask the Lord to open your eyes to a need within your current sphere of influence. What can you offer today to bring blessing and practical sustenance to that person or issue?

The whole house of Israel, all of them,
will serve Me in the land; there I will accept them.
EZEKIEL 20:40

*I know your deeds. Behold, I have put before you an
open door which no one can shut, because you have a little
power, and have kept My word, and have not denied My name.*
REVELATION 3:8

— Day 51 —

Known by His Stripes

He was wounded for our transgressions, He was bruised
for our iniquities; the chastisement for our peace
was upon Him, and by His stripes we are healed.
ISAIAH 53:5 NKJV

've been told that a mother zebra will separate her young foal from the herd for a period of time so that he can learn the unique shape of her stripes. She wants her offspring to be so well acquainted with the intricate nuances and patterns on her body that he will never mistake her for one of the other animals in the group. Every waking minute of those early days in his life are spent alongside her, becoming intimately familiar with the stripes that are his to keep returning back to—for protection, for caring, for everything he needs.

Our Savior has borne "stripes" for us. Every lash He endured, every blow, every beating, every strike against His body—they were all for us. The weight of our sin provided the impetus and momentum behind every weapon that gashed into His flesh. Our guilt was the gravity that pressed into His heart and sagged from His spirit. Yet within each wound lay the catalyst for our healing. His blood paid our impossible debt. Those scars absorbed our shame and replaced it with His righteousness.

So we remember them; we learn from them . . .

His stripes . . .

When we sit with Him in still moments—away from the busyness, the endeavors, the ongoing responsibilities of our lives—and simply see Him as He is, we become better acquainted with His undying love expressed to each of us in the stripes He bore on our behalf. In these quiet times, He separates us from anything and anyone who would vie for our devotion so that we can better know Him—this One who loves us and has paid the price for us. It's why He beckons us to come close, closer, closer still . . . where even a noisy, competitive world of distractions cannot keep us from seeing Him and His stripes with our full attention. Learning. Remembering. Those stripes tell our story. They hold our life's promise. They're like nothing else we've ever seen or known.

In His presence we are taught and changed and healed . . . "by His stripes."

Moments like these are priceless, when you're reminded of the price He paid, the wounds He endured, the blood He shed on your behalf. Staying acquainted with His stripes inspires you to repentance, reminds you of the mercy and freedom made available to you, replaces your despair with hope, your discouragement with a holy fervor.

> These stripes tell our story. They're like nothing else we've ever seen.

Other desires may come along throughout the day, promising that they alone are able to provide what we need. But having spent time observing His stripes, those loves aren't so adept at misleading or deceiving. False gods may try to trick us into the shallow existence they promise, but our love for Him, in response to His lavish love for us, will be too devoted to be divided. His stripes keep us safe and secure.

Look again today on the stripes He suffered. For you. Study them so you never forget them. And come back here again (and again) to make sure you never do.

Let us know, let us pursue the knowledge of the LORD.
HOSEA 6:3 NKJV

— He Speaks to Me —

Take time to worship Him for the depth of His love for you, expressed through the price He paid on your behalf.

He Himself bore our sins in His body on the cross,
so that we might die to sin and live to righteousness;
for by His wounds you were healed.
1 PETER 2:24

A better hope is introduced, through which we draw near to God.
HEBREWS 7:19 CSB

For Example

꙾

*Then Solomon and all the assembly with him went to the high
place which was at Gibeon, for God's tent of meeting was there.*
2 CHRONICLES 1:3

Leadership is not reserved for official, institutional positions,
recognized by title and business card. If you're a parent,
you're a leader. If you interact with others at work, church,
or anywhere people gather for shared purposes, your life creates
an impact. No matter what seat you occupy, if there is another
individual looking to you for direction, even just one, you're
operating from a seat of leadership.

That's why, as we study and glean from God's Word, we
shouldn't only be looking for those things that speak to us as
individuals and to our personal needs, but also transformative
insights into what successful leadership of others looks like. One
of these principles comes from the unexpectedly obscure scenery
of 2 Chronicles, right at the beginning of Solomon's reign. Mark
it well: he didn't just *tell* people what to do; he *led* them in what
to do.

He didn't just *point* them to Gibeon. He went *with* them.

As king, Solomon was a leader of leaders, giving them instructions on how he expected them to operate within their specific
spheres of influence. "Solomon spoke to all Israel," verse 2 says,
"to the commanders of thousands and of hundreds and to every
leader in all Israel." We're not told exactly what he shared with
his leaders that day, but we do know what happened next: they all
went to make burnt offerings to the Lord (v. 3) . . . with Solomon
at the head of the traveling party. They didn't go because they
were *sent*; they went because he led the way. They went "with
him." He took them there.

Leadership is never measured by what you say so much as the direction you choose to go. The example you're setting: Is it worth emulating? The course you're on: Is it a good one to follow? Important questions . . . because the patterns of responsibility and character you set (whether you realize it or not) will form a pathway that others will walk.

Are you modeling a diligent work ethic? Do your habits inspire others to faithfulness and good stewardship? Does a wrinkle in your day cause you to panic and complain, or does your example instead lead people toward faith and confidence in God's ability to handle problems?

> ## The patterns you set will form a pathway that others will walk.

What your children see in you, they register and remember. What others see patterned in your life, they internalize and file away. So don't just tell them what you think is right or what you want them to do. Show them as you "walk in a manner worthy of the Lord" (Col. 1:10).

Don't just send them out. Lead them.

Let no one look down on your youthfulness,
but rather in speech, conduct, love, faith and purity,
show yourself an example of those who believe.
1 TIMOTHY 4:12

— He Speaks to Me —

Who are some of the people you strive to pattern your life
after? How has their example impacted you? What do you want
your example to say and set for others?

If I then, the Lord and the Teacher, washed your feet,
you also ought to wash one another's feet.
John 13:14

The things you have learned and received and heard and seen in me, practice these things, and the God of peace will be with you.
PHILIPPIANS 4:9

Built for Abundance

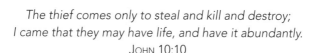

The thief comes only to steal and kill and destroy;
I came that they may have life, and have it abundantly.
JOHN 10:10

If any single phrase of Scripture is meant to capture the essence of what our experience with Christ is meant to be like, *abundant life* says it better than anything else, in twelve little power-packed letters.

Most of us believe in it—in theory—in the abundant, ever-filling, overflowing life that Jesus came to offer us. We believe it's hopefully waiting for us out there somewhere, at some point . . . if we could ever get past this bump in the road. *If* we could ever just feel better for a long enough stretch of time. *If* we could put this circumstance behind us, or pay our car off, or get through this wedding, or find steady work, or lose the weight we're struggling with. We think *if* we can just make it till the end of this year and turn the corner on a new one, we'll be ready for it. We can see it out there, once we're not so tied up with what's here.

Abundant life, here we come . . . *if.*

It turns out, however, abundant life is not something you experience in the absence of difficult, trying, challenging situations. Abundant life is what Jesus offers you right in the middle of them. Abundant life is something the Spirit enables you to have when all else is wrong, disheveled, or uneasy around you. This, in fact, is the state in which His abundance is best seen and experienced.

"The thief"—the Devil—is bent on using difficulties to "steal" from you, to "kill and destroy" your peace and confidence, so that you're consistently waiting on abundance *if* and when things change. His sinister tactic keeps you focused on all that is wrong, blinded to your current access to abundance. And yet because of Christ and your intimate relationship with Him, your heart—your entire life—can still be overwhelmed with an inexplicable, simultaneous hope and peace-filled stability, even when all else is disheveled around you.

Abundant life is the smile that creeps to the corners of your lips when God fills your heart with a peace that runs contrary to your reality. Abundant life is the sense of divine adventure that pulsates in your soul, even while you're sitting in a square, gray cubicle doing a job that comes nowhere close to tapping your potential. As soon as you tap into the available, Spirit-empowered reservoir that is a fountain of living water bubbling up inside, He raises a banner of hope in your heart and mind. As you trust Him to do this, something called abundant life actually shows up, right in the middle of the dreariness.

> Your God is here. Your God is able. And He has brought with Him abundant life.

Your marriage may be hanging by a thread; your finances may be a disaster; your child may be living a reckless, rebellious lifestyle; your doctor may have shown you an X-ray you never wanted to see with your name on it. But your God is here. Your God is able. And He offers abundant life, ready to be brought to the regular rhythms of your life right now, in this, in you.

Believe it.

And live in light of it today.

In Your presence is fullness of joy;
in Your right hand there are pleasures forever.
PSALM 16:11

— He Speaks to Me —

What evidence and hints of "abundant life" have you been ignoring in the midst of your current circumstances? What would walking in Christ's abundance and living by His Spirit look like today? Ask the Lord to allow the swell of His life in your life today.

All the streams of Judah will flow with water,
and a spring will issue from the LORD's house.
JOEL 3:18 CSB

*He gives strength to the weary, and to him
who lacks might He increases power.*
ISAIAH 40:29

All-Day Protection

--- ✤ ---

Even Satan disguises himself as an angel of light.
2 CORINTHIANS 11:14

Summer is known for its blazing hot sunshine, greeting you with a stinging salutation the moment you step outside. But sometimes a smattering of white clouds may arrive, parading slowly across the sky. And if they're big enough, and close enough together, they provide what feels like a canopy of relief from the shriveling effects of direct sunlight. In these conditions, you might decide to stay out on the playground or the beach a little longer than usual. Hold off on that extra application of sunscreen. Leave your visor and glasses inside, figuring the shade is sufficient cover, a trusted guard against overexposure.

And yet that cloud cover is misleading. Its skimpy filter cannot completely contain the effects of the sun's intense light. Its ultraviolet strength may be invisible, but it is powerful and cannot be diminished by passing attempts to dilute its energy. In fact, the sun damage to human skin is most pervasive when cloud cover prevails, when we think it's not working hard enough to be worried about, when we've worn no sunscreen and taken no precautions. The conditions outside may be cooler and less glaring. More comfortable, less worrisome. But the sun's harmful rays invisibly penetrate the gauze of visible clouds, and skin can be seared and burned, damaged and diseased. In actuality, the disguise makes the sun's work more potent and its heat more injurious.

Not unlike the way Satan disguises himself . . . and his dangers.

There are days, of course—and certain times or scenarios—when you more easily see, sense, and expect his withering rays of temptation. You can feel the heat of his schemes against you bearing down on the back of your neck. So you take precautions. You slather yourself in prayer and Scripture, dressing for the occasion in your spiritual armor.

But at other times, when you're feeling steady and secure in your faith and the cloud cover of good times have lulled you to sleep, you no longer sense the need to do as much proactive safeguarding. Your marriage is reasonably strong, your finances steady, your children safe, your own hang-ups somewhat silent for the moment. So you relax your pursuit of holiness and the priority you place on spiritual things.

In fact, the sun damage to human skin is most pervasive when cloud cover prevails.

But the smokescreen of happier times, even just normal times, shields the brazenness of his strategy, hoping to catch you unaware. You may not hear the clink of weapons being aimed your direction. You may not think the situation requires as much preparation and protection. You may be too tired or too comfortable to be concerned about being overly watchful.

That's when he'll burn you.

So today, plan ahead and pack spiritual supplies to keep his intentions at bay. Don't overlook the shady, innocuous spots. Even there, apply your spiritual sunscreen at full strength—so you can come home blessed and believing, instead of blistered and beleaguered.

Be of sober spirit, be on the alert. Your adversary, the devil,
prowls around like a roaring lion, seeking someone to devour.
1 PETER 5:8

— He Speaks to Me —

What kind of situations cause you to become less watchful and alert? What do you need to put in place to keep from being susceptible to sneak attacks?

*Let us not sleep, like the rest, but let us stay
awake and be self-controlled.*
1 THESSALONIANS 5:6 CSB

Keep watching and praying that you may not enter into temptation; the spirit is willing, but the flesh is weak.
MATTHEW 26:41

And . . . Action!

✦

When Jesus went ashore, He saw a large crowd,
and He felt compassion for them because
they were like sheep without a shepherd.
MARK 6:34

The disciples didn't feel like being too welcoming to the crowd waiting for them on the shoreline that day. They'd only barely caught their breath from an intense time of ministry and were still extremely exhausted, most likely looking for a place where they could put their feet up and rest. They probably hoped Jesus would do them all a favor and just send the needy multitude away instead of making this day last any longer.

And yet His response was the opposite of what naturally welled up inside His disciples. Jesus not only tolerated the people's presence. He opened Himself up to them. He moved Himself toward them. To help them.

"He felt compassion for them."

Compassion is one of the distinguishing characteristics of our God. All throughout Scripture we see it on display—from the father of the prodigal son running out to greet his wayward boy, to Jesus being moved to tears at the grave of his friend Lazarus before resurrecting his lifeless body. And on this particular day, surrounded by such a large and hungry crowd, it's what made Him willing to welcome the multitude that even His own disciples were hoping to wish away.

Compassion is not the same thing as sympathy. While the latter is a building block to the former, compassion does more than merely *feel*. It *compels*. It takes *action*. When Spirit-led compassion begins stirring in your heart, it prompts a response, not merely a sense of sadness or pity. Compassion is what caused the Good Samaritan, for example, to stop in the middle of his journey, delay his own plans, and tend to the needs of the wounded man who'd been beaten and left for dead by roving thieves. Compassion is willing to be inconvenienced. Compassion compels.

When was the last time you felt stirred in your heart toward the issues someone else was struggling to handle—enough to move toward them and help them? Perhaps, like the disciples, you're often fatigued by the load of cares and responsibilities that you are already carrying. But if you and I truly want to follow the example of Jesus, we'll step ashore into each new day with our radar up for where other people are hurting and in need. We'll see the stewardship of our time as an opportunity to put His love into practice. Even in the midst of our routine schedule, compassion will signal us toward a person who needs a minute to talk, or needs a prayer spoken over them, or needs the money we'd brought for lunch, or needs the smile of a caring friend.

> Compassion is willing to be inconvenienced. Compassion compels.

Ask the Lord to break your heart for what breaks His, and then ask Him to stir in you a sense of active compassion that makes you too uncomfortable to sit by and do nothing.

You heard from heaven, and according to Your great compassion You gave them deliverers who delivered them from the hand of their oppressors.
NEHEMIAH 9:27

— He Speaks to Me —

What needs or people has compassion signaled you toward recently? How have you responded?

_____

_____

_____

_____

_____

_____

_____

_____

_____

_____

_____

_____

*The Lord will vindicate His people, and will have compassion on
His servants, when He sees that their strength is gone.*
DEUTERONOMY 32:36

As those who have been chosen of God,
holy and beloved, put on a heart of compassion,
kindness, humility, gentleness and patience.
Colossians 3:12

— Day 56 —

Upward and Onward

*Jehoshaphat was afraid and turned his attention to seek
the LORD, and proclaimed a fast throughout all Judah.*
2 CHRONICLES 20:3

Likely, you know how it feels to be surrounded on all sides with difficulty and trouble. Wave after wave, from one day to the next, pummeling you with unrelenting, compounding trouble. You know what it's like to feel hemmed in from all directions, suffocating under the heaviness of life's issues, growing more weary and wary and increasingly afraid that you're never going to get through it in one piece.

One layer of hardship was enough. *But this too? Now?*

The steep repair bill was devastating enough. *But now the lost job too?*

The trouble you're having with your child is consuming enough. *But now the negative doctor's report too?*

The new responsibilities at work are enough. *But now increased business travel for your spouse too?*

Betrayal by your closest friend was heartbreaking enough. *But now you've been overlooked by another person in a hurtful way too?*

Surrounded. On all sides.

This is how King Jehoshaphat must have felt when "the Moabites and Ammonites, together with some of the Meunites" descended as a multi-headed force against Judah (2 Chron. 20:1 CSB). Not one but three marauding armies encroaching upon his land and his people, threatening their safety and security, terrorizing them with ominous threats, everywhere they turned their gaze.

Understandably then, fear crept up the spine of the king, who was manning a city under siege while everyone was looking to him for direction and inspiration. But even in an era when commitment and allegiance to God was rare, Jehoshaphat did what all people fighting battles on multiple fronts should do. He shifted his eyes away from the opposition, and instead he "turned his attention to seek the LORD." Instead of shrinking back, hiding, running for cover, and seeking escape, he turned his attention upward toward God as his way of moving forward. And He didn't stop there—he directed others to do the same.

When trauma or difficulty threatens your sense of calm and capability, resist the urge to let fear overwhelm you. While you may understandably *feel* fear (you're human, after all), the choice is yours whether or not you'll entertain it, wallow in it, and allow it to cripple you, letting it paralyze your forward movement. Assuage your emotional response with intentional, redirected attention. Focus on God, His promises, and His power to fight on your behalf against any army that threatens your borders—no matter how fierce, no matter how loud, no matter how many bases of operation they're shooting from.

The way to move onward is to shift your gaze upward. And He will carry you through.

> *Cast your burden upon the LORD and He will sustain you;*
> *He will never allow the righteous to be shaken.*
> PSALM 55:22

He turned his attention upward toward God as his way of moving forward.

— He Speaks to Me —

What can you do today to specifically and intentionally turn your attention upward to God and away from your difficulty? How will this shift in focus redirect the next steps you take?

The eyes of all look to You, and You give
them their food in due time.
PSALM 145:15

Humble yourselves under the mighty hand of God,
that He may exalt you at the proper time.
1 PETER 5:6

Signs and Wonders

❧

Here I am with the children the LORD has
given me to be signs and wonders in Israel.
ISAIAH 8:18 *CSB*

In the midst of delivering ominous, prophetic messages to his fellow countrymen for their sin and apostasy, Isaiah took one look at his sons and declared that these children were given as "signs and wonders." The prophet's offspring reminded him of the generational faithfulness of God, in spite of the nation's current state of spiritual apathy. Their existence meant the Lord was not finished with His people. In fact, He was still blessing them. Still giving from His heart to them. Still supplying evidence of a hopeful future for them.

Despite all they'd lost through their obstinacy and rebellion, His promises and blessings were still in effect. How did Isaiah know?

Because God was giving them children.

As "signs and wonders."

Your children are not only gifts, they are signs that point back to the promises and faithfulness of God to you. Others' children are signs of it too—the ones you see toddling along with their parents or grandparents at the park or the ball field or the shopping center. The ones you teach at the public school. The ones who call you aunt or uncle. Some days as we juggle the mundane duties of rearing children and managing the demands entailed—the dishes and the laundry, the school and sports and book reports—we lose sight of what these children of ours truly represent. When they're running around our feet, or whining for our attention, or making messes to be cleaned up, or requiring an errand that can't be easily fit into our schedule, we don't usually see our kids for what they are—living, breathing testaments of God's capacity for the miraculous. They are "signs and wonders" of His enduring, ever-replenishing nature, of His desire and ability to create fresh opportunities for His will to be done, generation after generation.

The gift of children means that He continues to have good plans for us. By embroidering them into the fabric of your family, or simply into your experience, children's mere presence makes a visible statement about God's character: His grace, His greatness, His generosity, His glory.

> The gift of children means that He continues to have good plans for us.

If we were running a world that was as troubling and complicating as ours, we would surely have shut down the whole operation a long time ago and considered it a lost cause. Dealing with people like us would be a terrible and persistent headache we didn't need. But God, being full of grace and mercy, and being a tender, long-suffering Father, declares He is not finished with what He started. Each new little being that enters the landscape of time and space from the hollow of His own hand is proof of it—proof that He is still taking His people toward a glorious and eternal conclusion.

So there's no need to doubt that God can still perform miracles for you—no need to worry that He's not up to something hopeful and special in your life. The daily proof is right there in front of your eyes.

Every child is a sign and wonder.

Permit the children to come to Me, and do not
hinder them, for the kingdom of God belongs to such as these.
LUKE 18:16

— He Speaks to Me —

What else are you perhaps overlooking amid the everyday? What other symbols of God's truth and goodness are intended for your ongoing encouragement?

He has remembered His covenant forever, the word which
He commanded to a thousand generations.
PSALM 105:8

Like newborn infants, desire the pure milk of the word,
so that you may grow up into your salvation.
1 PETER 2:2 CSB

Fan the Flame

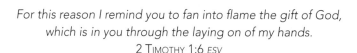

For this reason I remind you to fan into flame the gift of God,
which is in you through the laying on of my hands.
2 TIMOTHY 1:6 ESV

A gain and again, my brother walked back and forth from the bricked fire pit on the back patio to the spacious, wooded yard behind it, gathering specific kinds and sizes of fallen tree branches to put into the hollowed quarry. His wide-eyed nephews looked on, fascinated, admiring the manly craft of fire making. Mastery over the elements. Conquering the chill of nightfall by creating flame.

For unlike the artificial blaze inside the house, in the den fireplace, this fire would not brew and blossom with the flick of a switch. It wasn't automatic or coincidental, the quick combustion of spark and propane. This outdoor flame had to be carefully crafted and calculated. Manipulated and scrupulously tended. Its outcome depended on focused, intentional effort. This kind of fire wouldn't burn on its own.

Because fires like these take work.

The apostle Paul—mentor, father figure, kind pastor—spoke of this kind of fire when writing to a young, eager apprentice nearly two thousand years ago. He'd been examining the readied fire pit of Timothy's soul, the potential that God had placed inside him, the promise Paul had seen from firsthand observation. And he whispered a challenge in those pages that should still echo in the hearts of anyone who dares to live a life robustly alit for God: *Fan the flame,* he said to young Timothy. *Keep that flame burning bright.*

This same fire is in you as well—a holy fire, given and entrusted by God to every soul He's claimed as His own—the fire of His Spirit, emanating gifts and fruit, a bounty from God's abundance. This flame is built to burn away impurity, to refine treasure, to produce the kinds of activity that carry eternal reward. And yet this flame, if not tended and cared for, will wane and weaken in intensity. It will fail to emit the holy heat it's capable of generating. God has given you this fire, yes, but the hallowed task of keeping it fanned is your charge to accept. If you want to see your life roaring with spiritual energy, you must partner with Him in whipping it into a frenzy. You must invest in its continued rekindling—by pursuing a holy passion in prayer, by digging deeply into His written Word, by surrounding yourself with those whose fervency for Him is contagious and sincere, and by serving others in faithful obedience to Him.

> The hallowed task of keeping it fanned is your charge to accept.

Today's the day. The light is already aglow. The Father has graciously endowed you with a spiritual spark worthy of serving His kingdom and His people. The foundational work is already done. So when you see it growing dim, start fanning. When cold winds rush through the dark valleys of difficulty, start fanning. Don't accept a glowing ember when only a full blaze will do. Lean over that smoldering fire pit again.

And fan the flame.

*Practice these things; be committed to them,
so that your progress may be evident to all.*
1 TIMOTHY 4:15 CSB

— He Speaks to Me —

How can you tell when your internal fire is growing dim? What specific and intentional practices can you put in place today to fan the flame?

There is in my heart as it were a burning fire shut up
in my bones, and I am weary with holding it in.
JEREMIAH 20:9 ESV

Take diligent heed to yourselves to love the LORD your God.
JOSHUA 23:11

In Between

🌂
---

*They set out from Elim, and all the congregation
of the people of Israel came to the wilderness of Sin,
which is between Elim and Sinai.*
EXODUS 16:1 ESV

E lim is not a well-known stop on the Israelites' journey out of Egypt, but according to Exodus 15:27 (ESV), they found "twelve springs of water and seventy palm trees" in that little oasis. The people were able to make camp there. It was a refreshing respite in what had already become a thirsty walk, not long after crossing the Red Sea.

Sinai, of course, lay up ahead, and it would be an eventful place too. The Lord would give the Ten Commandments there and amaze them with His power visibly displayed on the mountain—fire, smoke, thunder, earthquake—awesome experiences that would show them the undeniable power of their God.

But "between" Elim and Sinai was a "wilderness"—barren, dry territory that left much to be desired. Here, they'd be put to the monotonous task of plodding along under a blazing hot sun while staring at endless acres of vast wasteland. But if they wanted to get to Sinai, to the things that God was preparing for them at that point in their journey, they'd need to be willing to forge through the landscape that led to it.

The in-between.

In-between times are necessary. They are the bridge between what He *has* done for you and what He's *preparing* to do in your future. This is the phase where you learn to draw close to Him, where He teaches you how to depend on Him for everything, even when another path seems preferable, and certainly more pleasurable.

Are you willing to go there? Willing to stay committed and faithful to the journey when there is nothing extraordinary to report? Willing to stay forward-facing when you're doing little else than putting one foot in front of the other, day after mundane day? Willing to keep up a sense of holy anticipation, eager to see what He has in store for you next, even when it doesn't feel like you're connecting with Him the way you once did?

Are you willing to dedicate yourself to the in-between, even when tempted to look back at the wonders of "Elim"—back when the movement of God was clearly flowing? When your prayer times were rich and vibrant? When spiritual disciplines didn't feel like such a chore, a duty, an effort? When your excitement at what He was doing was at a high crest?

> Are you willing to dedicate yourself to the in-between?

Perhaps at this moment, the wilderness feels as though it's draining you dry. The refreshment of Elim is no longer dripping off your tongue, nor is Sinai's peak in your line of sight. The stinging wind and dusty conditions, the high heat and low visibility—they're only intensifying your desire for what you wish your life could be right now. But trust God. Believe that if He has positioned you in-between for now, this is where you'll grow nearer to Him and where you'll be best prepared for what lies ahead.

The in-between time is not a waste. This phase in your journey will be worth your full engagement.

Elim was yesterday. Sinai is tomorrow.

But for now . . . *be* in-between.

You have need of endurance, so that when you have done the will of God, you may receive what was promised.
HEBREWS 10:36

— He Speaks to Me —

Describe your usual attitude and behavior during the in-between seasons of life. How can you handle them with renewed faith, trust, listening, and patience?

We count those blessed who endure.
JAMES 5:11

*Whatever was written in earlier times was written for
our instruction, so that through perseverance and the
encouragement of the Scriptures we might have hope.*
Romans 15:4

Not Quite So Quiet

---※---

While they were talking and discussing, Jesus Himself
approached and began traveling with them.
Luke 24:15

Perhaps "quiet time" to you has a certain ring to it, a certain mood. Early morning. All alone. Hot tea. Open Bible. Soft worship music playing in the background. Otherwise, sweet silence.

And while these moments are as wonderful as wonderful can be—times when you can just sit back and let God's Word pour into and over your spirit—life doesn't always accommodate this admirable ideal. Busy seasons at work, a virus bug running through the family, after-hours demands from ailing parents . . . they can all be downright disruptive to what you prefer as your favorite quiet-time conditions.

During times like these, your first inclination may be to simply hold off on meeting with the Lord until this bumpy patch passes, allowing you to get back into the swing of things once it's over. But even when this one clears up, there's no promise another one won't arise to take its place. This means if you confine God only to idyllic, quiet moments, you may have spoken with Him and heard from Him for the last time in a long time.

And that just won't do.

When life's pressures and unpredictability are at their peak, meet with Him anywhere you can. The Lord can amplify His Word in the school pickup line, with the engine running and your child due to arrive in five minutes. He can hear your hums of worship rising with the steam from your stovetop as you prepare dinner. He can respond to prayers in the elevator between the first-floor lobby and the fifteenth-floor board meeting. He is with you on *every* floor, same as when you're at home with your knees on your *own* floor.

When the alarm clock goes off in the morning, lie there for a few minutes and present your body as a living sacrifice, holy and acceptable to Him. Then as the day rolls on, intentionally listen for His voice. Turn your attention inward to see if the stirrings of His Spirit pique your attention even in the midst of your busyness. Keep His Word strategically positioned before you in the eventful places and spaces of life—stuck to your car dashboard and bathroom mirror, your kitchen sink and computer monitor. Speak silent blessings over your children as you're watching them practice or reading over their homework.

> We can meet with Him even in the midst of our distractions.

Jesus was known to meet people in the middle of the day's fishing business or while traveling on His way from one village to another. Who's to say these less conventional settings weren't every bit as memorable to the people who heard Him speak to them there as in places that seemed more conducive to spiritual conversation?

Yes, we need our quiet time with Him. But we also need Him and can meet with Him even in the midst of our distractions, so that we can respond and relate to them in a way that reflects His life in us. If today is "one of those days," if the time you've spent on this reading right now is truly all you can spare, take a verse, take permission, and know He'll be taking your hand all day long.

I shall lift up the cup of salvation and call
upon the name of the LORD.
PSALM 116:13

— He Speaks to Me —

Use one of the verses on these pages, or another one that God's Spirit brings to mind, to record and post in strategic places where you'll see it and can engage with it throughout your busy day.

If I take the wings of the dawn, if I dwell in the remotest part of the sea, even there Your hand will lead me, and Your right hand will lay hold of me.
PSALM 139:9–10

God is love, and the one who abides in love
abides in God, and God abides in him.
1 JOHN 4:16

The Father's Breath

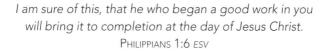

I am sure of this, that he who began a good work in you
will bring it to completion at the day of Jesus Christ.
PHILIPPIANS 1:6 ESV

Try as he might, my son couldn't force enough air from his full lung capacity to blow up the little red balloon he was trying to inflate. Dizzy from the strain, he collapsed into a chair in frustration, just as his father walked by and held out his hand. He took the balloon and started to work.

After four or five stretches of the latex material, he pressed the opening to his lips and gave it several strong blows, then cinched it between two fingers and handed the partially-filled balloon back. Our son looked confused. "You're not going to finish it? I've already tried and can't do it."

"You can now because I got it started. You can take care of the rest."

And sure enough he did, under his father's watchful gaze— amazed now that even his little-boy breath was able to enlarge the balloon to a full, rounded, taut-to-the-touch expanse. He handed it back to his dad for the final tie-off, and the work was completed.

The father's breath had broken the barrier to the impossible.

When the tasks of life are too tightly wound for our paltry resources to effect any lasting change, we are tempted to resort to more of our own effort. We inhale, we exhale, we give it all we've got—work our connections, perfect our résumé, exert our finest skill, invest money toward its success—only to be disappointed with the outcome, our best effort insufficient.

When will we learn to hand the thing over? When will we finally call on the One whose breath not only gives us life but is *in itself* the life behind everything we do? From up in the heavenlies, He infuses His plans for us with the catalytic propulsion of His divine power. We watch in stunned awe at the ease with which He sets things in motion—things we've been exhausting ourselves to try accomplishing for many years, through many tears.

But then He hands it back to us, assuring us that what we could not do then, we will be able to do now because He has initiated the work. And now He will empower us to roll on forward with it—completing the work *through* us, allowing us the privilege of partnering with Him. He knows we can't experience the full joy and purpose of what He's started by merely receiving from Him but not actively participating with Him. We don't garner new strength that way. We don't build sturdy character that way. He wants us to see our weakness mixing with His strength, causing our work to actually . . . work.

> The Father's breath is what breaks the barrier to the impossible.

Then when we've done all we can do, we don't let ourselves receive the accolade for what we know deep down belongs to the One who started this whole thing to begin with. So we hand it back to Him, letting Him seal it for all eternity. He takes our work. He ties the knot. And it is done.

Not by our might. Not by our power. But by the Spirit of God.

If the Spirit of Him who raised Jesus from the dead dwells in you, He who raised Christ Jesus from the dead will also give life to your mortal bodies through His Spirit who dwells in you.
Romans 8:11

— He Speaks to Me —

What have you been working hard to accomplish apart from the initiation of God's Spirit? On the other hand, what has He breathed upon that you've been too busy or too lazy to partner with Him in continuing?

_____

_____

_____

_____

_____

_____

_____

_____

_____

_____

_____

_____

The heavens were made by the word of the LORD,
and all the stars, by the breath of his mouth.
PSALM 33:6 CSB

He unleashes his winds, and the water flows.
PSALM 147:18 CSB

Dying to Live

─────────── ✤ ───────────

*Unless a grain of wheat falls into the earth and dies,
it remains alone; but if it dies, it bears much fruit.*
JOHN 12:24

In the spring and summer, many people go to their local home improvement store to buy plants, pine mulch, patio furniture, and lawn equipment in order to beautify their yards and outdoor living spaces during the warm weather months. So if you came at the end of the growing season, the varieties of plants and flowers would likely be slim, having been picked over by garden enthusiasts all summer long.

Yet you would still no doubt find a few remaining bags of simple grass seed in inventory. Still sitting there. The other bags that customers purchased throughout the year would have long ago been transformed into strong, healthy carpets of grass in neighborhoods all over town—growing, blossoming, flourishing. But the seeds that people *didn't* buy—the ones still contained in plastic bags, leaning up against the store wall—would all be hard and lifeless.

Because grass seed will forever remain grass seed until it's put into the ground.

And dies.

The difference is in the *dying*.

When grass seed enters the earth, the combination of water, nutrients, pollen, and other natural processes in the soil causes the seed's outer shell to peel away. To open up. To send out roots. To sprout. To grow. The seed husk dies so the plant can develop. If it won't stop being grass seed, it can never be grass.

Following Christ is a similar experience. The *potential* to flourish is there, but the *experience* of it hinges on the dying. If we don't die to old things so that we can produce new things, we won't see the kinds of changes in our everyday existence. If we as believers persist in worldly mind-sets and behaviors—in how we think and speak and react and entertain ourselves, in what we love and desire and dream about and wish to pursue—we, too, will miss out on the fresh, green blessings of transformation.

Living requires dying. Abundance requires yielding and relinquishing, surrendering and sacrificing. "The one who loves his life will lose it," Jesus said—while "the one who hates his life in this world will keep it for eternal life" (John 12:25 csb).

If it won't stop being grass seed, it can never be grass.

The option always exists for us to tolerate and stay attached to things that everybody else seems to be enjoying without any visible sign of loss, guilt, or diminishment. But time will show the consequences of hanging on to those little seed casings of comfort, complacency, and self-gratification. We'll see they only kept us from becoming what God truly created us for. But when we release our grip and sow our very lives, we give way to the new life that He can (and will) grow inside us and through us. For His glory.

If we have died with Christ, we believe
that we shall also live with Him.
Romans 6:8

— He Speaks to Me —

What are some of the seed husks you still keep around you, despite the limitations they place on your spiritual growth and freedom?

We always carry the death of Jesus in our body,
so that the life of Jesus may also be displayed in our body.
2 CORINTHIANS 4:10 CSB

If we live by the Spirit, let us also walk by the Spirit.
GALATIANS 5:25

Unstuck

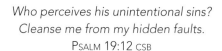

Who perceives his unintentional sins?
Cleanse me from my hidden faults.
Psalm 19:12 csb

I was driving along on a short trip to a ministry event, approaching a fairly large city that stood about halfway to my destination for the day, when I suddenly looked up and recognized I'd made a mistake. Though I was still on the right highway, I'd accidentally drifted into the HOV lane—the one reserved only for cars occupied by two or more people.

Getting out of the lane wasn't an immediate option. Concrete walls lined the driving space, preventing an easy return into the blended, main flow of traffic. To make matters worse, I could already see a police cruiser parked up ahead, obviously positioned to flag down people like me who take advantage of the less congested HOV lane to speed up their travel time.

I thought about sailing right past him. Maybe he'd be talking on his radio, filling out some paperwork, not paying attention to the passing cars at that split second. Maybe he wouldn't notice. Instead, I decided not to prolong the agony. I slowed to a stop behind him, gathered my papers from the glove compartment, and awaited his slow, stalking arrival.

When he stepped to my window, asking me what I needed, I admitted my fault—the accidental lane shift and my unfamiliarity with this roadway. Then I pointed around to my obvious lack of regulation passengers. My heart pounded as I awaited my punishment. But none came. Instead He smiled, actually thanked me for stopping, and then told me to hold out my hand. He took it in his, mildly slapped the back of it in a lighthearted manner, and said, "Okay, you're free to go now, ma'am. Be careful out there . . . and stay out of the HOV lane."

He was kind and gracious.

And so is God . . . because when we end up in a predicament without realizing it, and certainly without ever intending it, He responds to our repentance. Perhaps you've entered into what seemed like a sound relationship, or have procrastinated when you should have been preparing, or have unknowingly been creating a problem that only now has shown itself. And now you're walled in. You can't get loose. You didn't mean to get here, you *hate* being here, but . . . here you are.

> His heart toward us is to get us back on the road.

Listen, it's not too late. Because of the abundance of His mercy toward you and the tenderness of His heart, you can pull over right now. Even today, even after you're already this far down the road, He offers forgiveness and another chance. Like David, at the end of Psalm 19, ask forgiveness for "willful sins" (v. 13 CSB)—the ones you know about—but also for "unintentional sins" (v. 12 CSB), those things you didn't even detect as lapses in good judgment. Admit that you wish to be "blameless" and "acquitted" (v. 13).

Your Father will take your hand, like the kind police officer took mine. Yes, He will warn you against coming *back* here. And it is possible there may be a consequence to endure. But He will encourage you to retain the lesson you learned here. But then He will extend the gift of grace. Another chance. Another opportunity. His heart is to get you back on the road, back into serving Him, faithfully setting out on the journey again.

Unstuck.

> *Look upon my affliction and rescue me,*
> *for I do not forget Your law.*
> PSALM 119:153

— He Speaks to Me —

If you're stuck in one of those situations you never meant to get into, are you slowing down to receive His grace for a fresh start? If not, what's keeping you from it? Talk with Him about that today.

Be gracious to me, Lord, because I am in distress; my eyes
are worn out from frustration—my whole being as well.
PSALM 31:9 CSB

*Turn to me and be gracious to me, as is your
practice toward those who love Your name.*
PSALM 119:132 CSB

— Day 64 —

Life to the Fullest

God is able to make every grace overflow to you,
so that in every way, always having everything
you need, you may excel in every good work.
2 CORINTHIANS 9:8 CSB

Your God can be trusted.

He will grant you the full supply you need to excel at His purposes today, no matter how varied or prodigious those tasks may be. Every decision you need to make, every task you need to accomplish, every relationship you need to navigate, every element of daily life you need to traverse, God has already perfectly matched it up with an equivalent-to-overflowing supply of His grace.

And you must believe this . . . because whether or not you do will directly affect your ability to function out of this overflow in your daily life. When you truly believe that you will always have everything you need, and that because of His extravagant grace you will never lack, you'll be more willing and able to give freely of yourself and your resources, certain that God will always replenish your supply.

People who operate from a position of perceived lack and deficiency are stingy with their time, selfish with their resources, and tight-fisted with their energy. They're reluctant to sow of themselves into the lives of others, afraid they don't have enough to do it with—or that if they do, they won't have enough left over for themselves—enough time, energy, talent, money, skill, patience.

But whenever we operate that way, our truly important tasks and relationships of life—the ones that promise blessing to us as well as to others—go unattended and undone. Worse, we miss out on the privilege to fully participate in them, much less "excel" in them. When we don't feel as though we have the proper amount or type of resources, we recoil into a shell of insecurity instead of bursting with the power and provision of God. Therefore the "work" misses out on our touch. And we miss the many ways our "every good work" could touch *us*—the impact, the memories, the lessons, the experiences that God is knitting together to become a key part of our story.

This is why we must have confidence in His "overflowing" grace and provision and be content with what we have—because what He *has* given is what we need, and what He's sovereignly *withheld* isn't necessary to the completion of the task. Otherwise He'd have given it. Whatever He's given or not given, He's done for a specific reason—a reason known only to Him perhaps, but a reason you can trust with full confidence, sight unseen.

> Whatever He's given or not given, He's done for a specific reason.

When you choose to recognize this, fully trusting in His continued, abundant supply, you'll be able to engage in life in a way you never have before. You'll be living life to the fullest.

We pray for you always, that our God will count you worthy of your calling, and fulfill every desire for goodness and the work of faith with power.
2 THESSALONIANS 1:11

— He Speaks to Me —

Are there any ways in which you're behaving from a posture of lack and deficiency? How can you begin to proactively reverse your mindset and bring it into alignment with God's abundance?

You have put gladness in my heart, more than
when their grain and new wine abound.
PSALM 4:7

Instruct them to do good, to be rich in good works,
to be generous and ready to share . . . so that they
may take hold of that which is life indeed.
1 TIMOTHY 6:18–19

Distinguishing Freedom

❧

The LORD God commanded the man, "You are free
to eat from any tree of the garden."
GENESIS 2:16 CSB

The voice of God points to freedom. He wants you focused
on the abundance of living within His wise, loving framework of boundaries. He tells you, "You can!"—so that
even when His answer is "no," it still opens up the possibility
of greater opportunity and access. He leads you out of the rigid
and suffocating framework of the legalistic, into the wide-open
spaces of grace and freedom.

Notice from Genesis 2:16 what God told Adam and Eve.
They were "free" to eat from whatever tree they liked—with the
exception, of course, "from the tree of the knowledge of good
and evil" (v. 17). This tree alone was off-limits. But His instruction clearly pointed them toward freedom—potential, opportunity, possibility—toward what they *could* do.

When the serpent slithered into the conversation, however, he
distorted God's commands in a most strategic and sinister manner—a method that still marks many of his suggestions toward
us even to this day. "Did God really say, 'You can't . . . " (Gen.
3:1 CSB).

No, He really didn't. God hadn't said "you can't eat from
any tree in the garden," as the serpent alleged. But the Enemy
desperately wanted Adam and Eve to believe He had . . . because
the difference between freedom and restriction is the difference
between life and death. It's the difference between blessing and
loss.

The voice of the Enemy will always accentuate restriction. He'll say, "You can't." He manipulates God's direction, twisting it around to focus on what you *can't* have instead of what you *can*. He shines a spotlight on limitations because he knows it will heighten the attention you give to it. He wants to entice you to sadness over what's being withheld from you, rather than celebration over all that's been made available to you.

Duty and religion place undue wear and tear on the human soul. They burden and exhaust you instead of providing you with invigoration and renewal. But God's voice, coming clear to you by virtue of His relationship with you . . . that's a whole other story. His voice points to freedom; the Enemy's voice points to restriction.

> God's voice points to freedom; the Enemy's voice points to restriction.

So as you seek to discern God's guidance in life, ask yourself: Which of the options you're hearing are pointing toward and accentuating the abundance of all He's given you to be and do? Which one is free of fear, insecurity, and a sense of "I can't?" Which one loosens you, and which one suffocates you?

Which one . . . sets you free?

He has made us competent to be ministers
of a new covenant, not of the letter, but of the Spirit.
For the letter kills, but the Spirit gives life.
2 Corinthians 3:6 csb

— He Speaks to Me —

What's a decision you're facing, or perhaps just a daily struggle you're enduring, where you're focusing on the cost rather than the opportunity? Take time to express gratitude to your kind Father for the freedom He has offered you in Him.

It was for freedom that Christ set us free; therefore keep standing firm and do not be subject again to a yoke of slavery.
GALATIANS 5:1

He has sent me to bind up the brokenhearted,
to proclaim liberty to captives and freedom to prisoners.
Isaiah 61:1

All-Night Brightness

❦

Even the darkness is not dark to You, and the night is
as bright as the day. Darkness and light are alike to You.
PSALM 139:12

L ost in the silence and beautiful darkness of the evening
skies, in flight between London and Johannesburg, our
airplane continued its gradual rise toward cruising altitude
while I situated myself for a peaceful night of sleep. Then, all at
once, it happened. We burst through a layer of thick cloud cover
and were suddenly washed in full, stark sunlight. What only
moments before had been a black ocean of celestial ink instanta-
neously erupted into a stream of sunlight, glinting off the plane's
wingtips and blinding me through the opened window with
striking brilliance.

I instinctively raised a hand to cover my eyes, turning away
while retinas and pupils busily recalibrated their adjustments.
That's when I noticed the time display on a digital clock near the
front of the plane, still set to the time zone of our departure city.
The full irony of the scene registered slowly at first, then picked
up speed as the Holy Spirit did His work in my heart.

3:48 a.m. The middle of the night. We were in full sunlight
here, though these were the darkest hours of the night *there*.

As clearly as ever, I heard the voice of God whispering in
my spirit, reminding me of something that's actually an every-
night truth all over the world: "If I say, 'Surely the darkness will
overwhelm me, and the light around me will be night,' even the
darkness is not dark to You, and the night is as bright as the day.
Darkness and light are alike to You" (Ps. 139:11–12).

Even the darkest hours of the night—and of our lives—have a bright side in Him.

If the darkness is overwhelming you—the inky blackness of tragedy or difficulty stretching out before you, leaving a devastating stain on your life—remember the bright Light that still shines at the bleakest of times. You may not see the rays of His handiwork from this vantage point, but a simple shift in perspective will reveal the brightness of His hope penetrating the most ominous and threatening clouds. He does not cease being God when life is tough. He still reigns, still illumines, still shatters through the night with His glory.

So pivot your attention in the dark hour—when your problems seem heavier, your worries more overwhelming, your regrets all-consuming, your wounds more traumatizing. Remind yourself that although it may be midnight here, you live underneath the paradoxical wonders of His ongoing, never-ending, always-shining favor and grace that even the darkest nights cannot hold at bay. Turn your gaze away from what's frustrating you, frightening you, and stealing all your joy and confidence, and see this One through whom the Light pierces every disappointment. Even in your midnight hour, He is still vividly present—even when, especially when, it's the darkest you can imagine.

That night, flying over the Dark Continent, I learned it's not dark everywhere at 3:48 a.m. In fact, where God lives, it's not dark ever. I guess the way you see that hour just depends on the perspective you have when taking it in.

> Even the darkest hours of the night have a bright side in Him.

He knows what is in the darkness,
and the light dwells with Him.
DANIEL 2:22

— He Speaks to Me —

Chronicle some of the "paradoxical wonders" of His ongoing, never-ending, always-shining favor and grace that you still experience in the dark nights of life.

Can a man hide himself in hiding places so I do not see him?"
declares the LORD. "Do I not fill the heavens and the earth?"
JEREMIAH 23:24

The light shines in the darkness,
and the darkness has not overcome it.
JOHN 1:5 ESV

Ins and Outs of Prayer

---

*The whole multitude of the people were in prayer
outside at the hour of the incense offering.
And an angel of the Lord appeared to him.*
LUKE 1:10–11

Zechariah, a holy and devout man, was about to get the surprise of a lifetime while performing his priestly duties in the temple. "An angel of the Lord appeared to him," declaring a stunning message: God had heard his prayer and was prepared to answer it. Zechariah and his wife, Elizabeth, were old and had no children. But this couple, well past child-bearing years, was soon to have their first child—a son—whose name would be John, the forerunner of the Messiah. Zechariah and Elizabeth's lives—truly, all of our lives—would be changed forever.

But among the more interesting sidebars to this familiar story is a detail mentioned in verse 10. A large gathering of people were vigilant "in prayer outside" while Zechariah went about his duties inside, preparing the customary offering of incense.

Zechariah was serving *inside*; the people were praying *outside*.

The mention of this involvement and intermingling of parties is not mere coincidence, an insignificant observation on the part of the Gospel writer. Nor is it meant to be contained to this ancient event in Scripture.

Because serving matters.

And because prayer matters too.

While you are serving *inside* your home, your job, your ministry, or whatever place where you carry out your ongoing duties before the Lord, you need a concerned core of people who are *outside* those events and venues, lifting you up and keeping you covered in the task—just as you have the privilege to do for them when they are in the throes of investing in their own tasks.

The prayers of others are like an incubator that help shape a protective environment, one which gives the Enemy a harder time penetrating and troubling you with his temptations, deceptions, and distractions. Heartfelt intercessions form a cocoon where your attention can more fully maintain its focus on Him, on the freedom of doing your work, and on hearing Him speak to you in the midst of it. Fervent petitions by others—friends or even strangers—who want God's best for you can help usher in and facilitate many holy moments in your life and experience.

Sadly, modern times have elevated and promoted self-reliance as a primary virtue. In reality, however, we are stronger together—each person doing their part, one at work while another prays them through it. In this way we succeed together, until the roles reverse and we encircle the one who's putting their hands to the plow of a specific task. Each of us needs the faithful, watchful, servant-hearted care of brothers and sisters who can support us in prayer while we're investing ourselves in the projects that go along with our current seasons of life.

Who's "outside" praying for you today while you're in here?

Whether you realize it or not, you need prayers for your safety, effectiveness, usefulness, and openness in all the activities you undertake. Who's "outside" praying for you today while you're in here? Have you considered that their work is as important and needful as yours?

Brothers and sisters, pray for us.
1 THESSALONIANS 5:25 CSB

— He Speaks to Me —

Who are some of the people who already help incubate you inside their prayers? How could you proactively widen your prayer circle? Who are you being diligent to cover in prayer today?

Be on the alert with all perseverance and petition for all the saints.
Ephesians 6:18

We rejoice when we ourselves are weak but you are strong;
this we also pray for, that you be made complete.
2 CORINTHIANS 13:9

They Could Not

---※---

The disciples came to Jesus privately and said,
"Why could we not cast it out?"
MATTHEW 17:19 ESV

A devastated father fell to his knees before the Messiah. He explained in desperation that his beloved son was terribly sick, suffering from seizures and bouts of epileptic craziness. The father's heart broke for his child. He wanted, more than all else, to see him in good health.

The fact that we see this man positioned before Jesus when the narrative begins in Matthew 17 leads us to believe that he started his quest for healing here, in this moment, before the Healer. But Matthew quickly clears up the misconception by chronicling what this tearful father said to Jesus, how he'd already "brought him to your disciples, and they could not heal him" (v. 16 ESV).

They could not.

But they should have.

This father was not only desperate but also disappointed. His encounter with Jesus' closest companions had left his questions unanswered, his son unhealed, his heart still broken. Nothing had changed even though he'd encountered men for whom Jesus had given "authority over unclean spirits, to cast them out, and to heal every kind of disease and every kind of sickness" (Matt. 10:1). Even without the Messiah's physical presence, the disciples had been empowered to work the Messiah's wonders. An encounter with them should have been as fruitful as an encounter with Him.

Instead, what a shame . . . *they could not.*

You, adopted child, have been endowed with God's Spirit. You are a temple in which God's power and presence pulsates. This gift is not only intended to enable communion between you and your Father, but also to empower you to function as His hands and feet within your sphere of influence. Those who have yet to encounter Him should encounter His power *through you*. They should never leave your presence in a state of spiritual dissonance—saddened and discontented that their encounter with a Jesus follower left no proof of Jesus' power.

> Those who have yet to encounter Him should encounter His power in you.

Their deepest questions should find discerning answers.

Their practical needs should find generous solutions.

Their hurting heart should find empathetic compassion.

Their deadened soul should find redemption and reawakening.

Their entire lives should be touched by the supernatural . . . through you.

May there never be a solitary person to leave our presence saying of us, *They could not.* Because by His Spirit, we can. We must.

Today, may you recognize the power you've been given by the God of heaven to be the answer to someone else's prayer.

Not by your power. Not by your might.

But by the Spirit of God.

We have received, not the spirit of the world,
but the Spirit who is from God, so that we may
know the things freely given to us by God.
1 CORINTHIANS 2:12

— He Speaks to Me —

Are there any opportunities during this day where you can foresee having an opportunity to be a demonstration of the Spirit's power and presence to others? Ask the Lord to give you the faith and courage to follow through.

You will receive power when the Holy Spirit has come upon you.
Acts 1:8

By this we know that we abide in Him and He in us,
because He has given us of His Spirit.
1 JOHN 4:13

Obedience Is Better

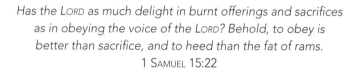

*Has the LORD as much delight in burnt offerings and sacrifices
as in obeying the voice of the LORD? Behold, to obey is
better than sacrifice, and to heed than the fat of rams.*
1 SAMUEL 15:22

While trapped in the fish's belly after failing to obey God's missionary call, Jonah promised the Lord, "I will sacrifice to You with the voice of thanksgiving. That which I have vowed I will pay" (Jonah 2:9). He was likely speaking of the thanksgiving or peace offerings prescribed in Leviticus 7. And obviously, nothing was wrong with Jonah's desire to return to Jerusalem and engage in these ceremonial rituals that God had commanded of His people. After what Jonah had done, you've got to be encouraged that he would seek to reengage with God in worship at all.

Except for one thing. God had told him to go to Nineveh, not Jerusalem. Despite pious intentions, Jerusalem was really in *Jonah's* direction, not *God's*. All the unleavened cakes and wafers in the world, glazed with dutiful brushes of olive oil, presented to the Lord in solemn, grateful praise and honor, could not do for Jonah what only his willing, surrendered obedience to the original assignment could accomplish. Making good by going to Nineveh was more important than making amends by going to Jerusalem.

Whenever we find ourselves at that uncomfortable crossroads where sin and consequences meet, the right response is always repentance. But repentance does not mean going off in a good direction; it means going in God's direction. And oftentimes, there can be a big difference.

Sometimes when we're caught red-handed in our rebellious running from God, we react by going to our Monday night Bible study again. More regularly, this time. We pray more. We give more. We fast through the day on Fridays. We commit to always saying a blessing over every meal, even in public, even when we're totally by ourselves. We do those pious things that make us feel more spiritual, renewed, connected with God again.

Good.

But God is seeking *relationship* with us, not simply a religious reaction from us. He prefers we get *right* with Him rather than just behave for Him. Because if we don't recognize the difference between the two, He knows we'll soon return to the same evasions and avoidances we'd been displaying before, even after we've said we're sorry and tried to patch things up with Him. We may be different, but not in the way that makes any lasting difference.

> God is seeking relationship with us, not simply a religious reaction from us.

The Devil is never far away, even when you're contemplating repentance. And if he fails at being able to lure you back into the comforts of sin, he's just as happy if he can tempt you into choosing a more comfortable, even more admirable method of avoiding obedience—something that *feels* like repentance, even if it's not exactly what God is asking you to do.

Is there an area of your life where you've run from God and are now seeking restoration? Don't assuage your conscience with a litany of rigorous religious activity. Seal your repentance with a surrendered heart willing to go in whatever direction He asked you to go in the first place.

The sacrifices of God are a broken spirit; a broken and a contrite heart, O God, You will not despise.
PSALM 51:17

— He Speaks to Me —

What has the Lord asked you to do or not do? If you've avoided these directives, pursue repentance and then renew your commitment to obedience today.

_____

_____

_____

_____

_____

_____

_____

_____

_____

_____

_____

_____

The sons of Israel walked forty years in the wilderness . . .
because they did not listen to the voice of the Lord.
JOSHUA 5:6

Behold, the Lord's hand is not so short that it
cannot save . . . but your iniquities have made
a separation between you and your God.
Isaiah 59:1–2

Stormy Detours

---⚜---

A fierce wind called the "northeaster" rushed down from the island. Since the ship was caught and unable to head into the wind, we gave way to it and were driven along.
Acts 27:14–15 csb

Surely no long sailing voyage was ever completely without incident in the first century, but the one carrying Paul and other prisoners bound for Rome was devastating by anyone's measure. The wind kicked up at some point in their journey and wouldn't relent, creating weeks of harrowing turbulence and heroic attempts at rescue. Finally, in a last-ditch effort at not capsizing on the high seas, they ran aground near the island of Malta, where they swam ashore on floating planks and other pieces of debris that once had been their traveling vessel.

Malta was not their original destination. But Malta was where they ended up.

Storms will do that to you sometimes—wash you ashore in unfamiliar places, around unfamiliar people.

Paul and those with him were greeted there by the island residents. And he quickly discovered that this unexpected destination of Malta was teeming with opportunity for ministry. "The leading man of the island" (Acts 28:7) had a father who'd been put to bed with fever and sickness. Paul went and prayed over him, and the man received healing from his condition. "After this, the rest of those on the island who had diseases also came and were healed" (v. 9 csb). If not for the storm, Paul wouldn't have been in this location to meet these people and help them.

But God's sovereignty had not been shipwrecked by the storm. His plans were not derailed just because the sailors' plans had been thrown off course. God's hand had steered them to the exact place where revival was primed to break out. And the storm was the instrument He used to do it.

Think of how long the people of Malta had been calling out, begging for help from their distresses—praying to their gods, perhaps wondering if there even *was* a God. They could not have known that the answer to their prayer was being brewed up by a storm. For out on the ocean where Paul was also praying, confident that God was somehow going to bring him safely to *his intended* destination, the Lord was diverting him to this place where he would have the privilege of being God's answer to someone else's prayers.

> God's sovereignty had not been shipwrecked by the storm.

Are you in a fierce storm right now? Are you watchful and mindful of the various places it's unexpectedly taking you and all the various people it's unexpectedly introducing you to?

Next time you're frustrated or perplexed by where your latest storm has dumped you, pray for the joy of discovering that God is using this storm to intersect your life with someone else's life, becoming part of answering *their* prayer, even as He's answering yours. Pray that He would make you sensitive enough, discerning enough, and interested in other people enough to sense when He is moving you into position to be a caring solution to their need.

Because not even a storm can reroute God's people from being a key part of God's purposes.

*Even if I am being poured out as a drink offering
upon the sacrifice and service of your faith,
I rejoice and share my joy with you all.*
PHILIPPIANS 2:17

— He Speaks to Me —

Where is an unlikely place that a personal storm has taken you? What were some of the potential touch points it provided you into others' lives?

Rejoice in hope; be patient in affliction; be persistent in prayer.
Share with the saints in their needs.
ROMANS 12:12–13 CSB

. . . as sorrowful yet always rejoicing, as poor yet making many rich, as having nothing yet possessing all things.
2 CORINTHIANS 6:10

Unlikely Signs of Life

---※---

I will restore the captivity of My people Israel,
and they will rebuild the ruined cities and
live in them; they will also plant vineyards and
drink their wine, and make gardens and eat their fruit.
AMOS 9:14

The old tarnished mailbox hadn't received even so much as a credit card offer in years, much less a handwritten note or a cheery birthday card. From all appearances, it had been left standing—and rusting, its door agape—long since its owners had moved away or succumbed to old age.

I inched closer to it while walking along the country road, where it leaned on its metal post at an odd angle. I noticed first a loose collection of debris inside—but then a flutter and a burst of feathers, as a bird emerged from its dark hollows with a violent flapping of wings. I was startled. I wasn't expecting *that* to come from something as dilapidated as *this*. I looked again and discovered that a nest was in there, clutching tiny eggs encircled by carefully laid brush and sticks.

This old, stale, rusted mailbox had become the nesting ground for new life.

Is there a dark, deadened area of your life that you've been trying to close off and put behind you for as long as you can recall? Too many memories. Too much pain. A world of embarrassing moments and choices that would kill you if people knew. You've let this place age and harden and petrify. You don't want anyone pecking around in there, able to see how dented and damaged you've been, how unsightly and stained and misshapen. The only way to handle this part of your life, you've decided, is to pull the door shut, seal the opening, prevent anyone from making further entry or inquiry, and leave the darkness in charge to rule over and entomb it . . . because nothing good or hopeful can ever come from that place.

But what if you chose to at least leave the door open, accessible to the possibility of life in Christ? The old, rusted, lifeless places in our hearts can become the breeding ground for surprising opportunities for beauty and bounty, brimming with new life.

When we become willing to unseal the lid on them a bit, allowing God and His healing purposes to become involved, our broken places become birthing places, remarkably able to give people a surge of encouragement, the kind that might just inspire them to hope and trust in God again. His work in us demonstrates to them God's overcoming power to repurpose these ugly areas for His glory. It helps them see that their own damaged memories, cradled in His warm hands, can still hold signs of life.

> Damaged memories, cradled in His warm hands, can still hold signs of life.

What if the areas you want to keep hidden, believing it's the only way to protect yourself from humiliation or loss, are actually the very places where God wants to originate the most stunning miracles of all? What if your best opportunities to exclaim His greatness to others won't come from the pristine places but the rusty ones that have received a fresh touch from His Spirit inside?

He can do it in you . . . and then through you.

Life can stir from the most unlikely places, if only you'll open yourself up to Him again.

Make me to hear joy and gladness,
let the bones which You have broken rejoice.
PSALM 51:8

— He Speaks to Me —

What are some of the strained places in your life that you've kept locked up and unattended? What's your real motive for keeping them hidden? Spend time in prayer asking God to give you the courage to open these places up to Him again.

I will place the juniper in the desert together with the box tree and the cypress, that they may see and recognize, and consider and gain insight as well, that the hand of the LORD has done this.
ISAIAH 41:19–20

I will not die, but live, and tell of the works of the LORD.
PSALM 118:17

Just One Look

❧

Mary Magdalene came, announcing
to the disciples, "I have seen the Lord."
JOHN 20:18

Mary Magdalene came to the tomb of Jesus early in the morning, "while it was still dark" (John 20:1). Hopes dashed. Life, as she knew it, over. What she found, however, was even worse than the horror she'd already endured. The stone that had sealed Jesus' grave was now missing. Someone had stolen Him, it seemed. His body, already ravaged by the torture He'd undergone, was now apparently being subjected to even further indignities.

And so she wept. She felt the piling on of despair. She'd seen the horrors of the crucifixion unfold and was certain that it couldn't possibly get any worse. And yet it did. It had. It was. The pain was becoming even more painful. The devastation was growing even more devastating. On top of everything else, she'd been robbed of the common decency of closure. Whatever finality she had begun to make of Jesus' horrifyingly public death was slipping from her grasp.

No one knew or could tell her what had become of Him. The angels in the white clothing, though certainly a shock to her senses, didn't offer any specific answers. Neither did the man who appeared to be the gardener, standing there, seemingly oblivious, asking who she was looking for.

But as she gazed off into the perplexing, impossible distance, she heard this mysterious "gardener" say simply, "Mary." There was only one person who said her name like that. Only One who called it with such a beautiful cadence of love, forgiveness, grace, and hope. So at once, "she turned" (v. 16). And when she did, everything changed.

In turning to that voice, her gaze brought her face-to-face with the brilliance and beauty of the risen Christ. In changing her perspective and reorienting her focus, everything became revolutionized—her morning, her outlook, her future, her whole life. Despair dissolved into hopeful joy because "she turned" from an empty tomb of disappointment to the full embodiment of the risen Savior. Despite everything now, she could rush to tell His disciples, "I have seen the Lord" (v. 18).

> "She turned." And when she did, everything changed.

"Fixing our eyes on Jesus" is not just an inspiring line of memory verse (Heb. 12:2). In turning to Jesus, we can be freed from our crippling fear and inner torment. In turning to Jesus, we can "lay aside" all the weight we're carrying—the hurts, the sins, all the accumulated pressures of life. In turning to Jesus, we're able to "run with endurance" through situations that are often difficult but, because of Him, can never be defeating. "Eyes on Jesus" is the Bible's proven antidote to growing weary, to losing heart, to giving up, to going down (vv. 1–3).

Whatever difficulty may be devastating or displacing you today, turn to Jesus again. And find the Resurrection answer that renews, restores, and redirects the entire course of your life.

> *I thank my God always concerning you for
> the grace of God which was given you in Christ Jesus.*
> 1 CORINTHIANS 1:4

— He Speaks to Me —

Where do you usually look when you're at the lowest points in life? What can you do to "turn to Jesus" in a practical way today?

_____

_____

_____

_____

_____

_____

_____

_____

_____

_____

_____

As it is, we do not yet see everything
subjected to him. But we do see Jesus.
HEBREWS 2:8–9 CSB

Rejoice as you share in the sufferings of Christ, so that you may also rejoice with great joy when his glory is revealed.
1 Peter 4:13 csb

He Took Our Place

When the sun had set and it was dark, a smoking
fire pot and a flaming torch appeared and
passed between the divided animals.
GENESIS 15:17 CSB

*I*n ancient times the foundation for relationship between two people or groups of people was established through a binding agreement known as a *covenant*. So when God sought to establish permanent relationship with His people through the bond He'd initiated with Abram, He didn't stop at a verbal exchange. He used the elements of covenant that were already present and understood within culture to ensure Abram of the authenticity and gravity of what He was establishing.

In those days, in order for a contract between two participants to be sealed, an animal would sometimes be killed, cut in two, and laid to either side. Then both parties in the agreement would walk between the pieces of dismembered animal remains—a visible statement of undying loyalty to the other party. The translation of this act was clear: If either person, tribe, or nation ever committed treason against the other, they could expect their lives and families to be torn apart, just as the animal's carcass had been.

In Genesis 15:9–10, Abram would have known he was responsible to walk between the halved animals, but God caused him to fall into a deep sleep. And then, in one of the most incredible theophanies in all the Old Testament (moments when God Himself appeared in a physical manifestation), the Lord passed between the animal pieces Himself, represented by a smoking pot of fire and a flaming torch. Not only did God do His own part in the covenant ceremony, He also did Abram's part. *God took Abram's place.* He assumed the full weight for the covenant's fulfillment onto His own divine shoulders.

It wouldn't be up to Abram to keep his relationship with God intact. He could simply trust Yahweh to be the covenant keeper, and it would be "credited" to Abram "as righteousness" (v. 6). God knew He'd be the only One capable of fully keeping the terms of the agreement. So in an act of extravagant grace and mercy, He laid claim to the wages of His people's future treason.

And what He did for Abram (Abraham) then, He has done for us now through His Son. Hallelujah!

> In an act of extravagant grace and mercy, He laid claim to the wages of His people's future treason.

While we were asleep in our trespasses and in our sins, Jesus passed through the gauntlet on our behalf, accepting both the penalty for our sin as well as the responsibility for keeping us secured with Him in relationship. He has assumed the entire cost of the covenant, and we live now in the blessings of what He came to accomplish.

Knowing the bottomless pit of love and grace that He has bestowed upon our frail humanity should compel an outburst of gratitude and a continued allegiance throughout this day. And every day for the rest of our lives.

He made Him who knew no sin to be sin on our behalf,
so that we might become the righteousness of God in Him.
2 CORINTHIANS 5:21

— He Speaks to Me —

Spend some time in worship today, praising the One who took your place.

If the inheritance is based on law, it is no longer based on a promise; but God has granted it to Abraham by means of a promise.
GALATIANS 3:18

*It is by grace you have been saved, through faith—
and this not from yourselves, it is the gift
of God—not by works, so that no one can boast.*
EPHESIANS 2:8–9 NIV

Helmet On

Since we belong to the day, let us be
self-controlled and put on the armor of faith and love,
and a helmet of the hope of salvation.
1 Thessalonians 5:8 csb

Whenever a football player's helmet comes off his head during the game—even if it's knocked off in the heat of the action—the established regulations demand that he sit out for a play. If he wants to get back in the game, he must first go to the sidelines, check his equipment, tighten his chin-strap, be sure nothing's loose, firmly reposition his headgear, and then—*then*—he can reenter the contest. Not *before* then. The helmet is so essential to his safety, to his ability to perform anything successfully on the ball field, he cannot risk having his head unprotected for even a single play or portion of a play.

The helmet of salvation, of course, is even more essential. *Much* more essential. Inherent within it are all the truths regarding your spiritual identity in Christ, as well as the ongoing, eternal inheritance you've been given as a child of God to experience and utilize here on the earth. Your helmet is loaded with the biblical realities that serve as crucial safeguards while you traverse the difficult, ongoing realities of each day.

Your opponent is crafty. His sinister intentions, demonic. He'll seek to cripple you with lies and strongholds that will keep you from reaching the goal of your God-given destiny. But with your helmet securely in place, you can block his advances. When he seeks to slow you down by convincing you that you are unloved, unlovable, unworthy of anything good or redemptive, it is your helmet of salvation that fortifies you with the reminder that you've been chosen and adopted and loved with an everlasting love.

When he suggests that you are not forgiven, and perhaps unforgivable, your helmet of salvation helps you fight back with assurances that your sins are not only covered by the mercy of God, but you are free of all condemning charges against you—past, present, or future—and cannot be separated from the love of the Father, either now or ever.

When you're feeling the fatigue of spiritual battle, as well as a sense of comparison and inferiority to other people, your helmet of salvation impresses upon you the reality that you are firmly rooted in Jesus, that you are seated with Him in heavenly places, and that you have been created and equipped to bear fruit for His glory.

> The helmet of salvation represents all the high-value items that are yours in Christ.

The helmet of salvation, positioned to a snug fit, represents all the high-value items that are yours in Christ. If you narrow your view of salvation to only include its eternal ramifications, you'll never experience all the staggering practical and present benefits that are meant to be yours. You need its full coverage *now* so your mind will not be exposed and unprotected against the schemes of the Enemy.

So when you're out there in the middle of the warfare today, and you realize his lies are beginning to infringe onto your territory, don't try to keep playing without your helmet on. Take a moment to go to the sidelines and secure the realities of your salvation into their proper place. Your helmet is there. Always. Ready to protect you in the heat of battle. Don't go anywhere without it.

The Lord is faithful, and He will strengthen
and protect you from the evil one.
2 Thessalonians 3:3

— He Speaks to Me —

Begin keeping a list of some biblical reminders that confirm who you are in Christ. How well-fitted is your helmet of salvation for action today?

Whatever is true, whatever is honorable, whatever is right,
whatever is pure, whatever is lovely, whatever is
of good repute, if there is any excellence
and if anything worthy of praise, dwell on these things.
PHILIPPIANS 4:8

We have obtained an inheritance,
having been predestined according to His purpose
who works all things after the counsel of His will.
Ephesians 1:11

Lightening the Load

———————— ✤ ————————

*All things are lawful for me, but not all things are profitable. All
things are lawful for me, but I will not be mastered by anything.*
1 CORINTHIANS 6:12

Marathon runners are known for their athletic physiques—
thinly chiseled frames that testify to lots of green, leafy
vegetables, rugged exercise, and at least eight full glasses
of water every day. And while there are some marathoners who
break the body-image stereotype, none of them deviates from
one clear distinctive: their uniform while running a race. Each of
them wears an airy, light, and cool outfit that might be unique
in color but similar in style . . . because no serious runner wants
to be bogged down with weighty clothes or unnecessary gadgets.
They keep it simple, keep it minimal. They don't want anything
on their bodies that adds increased mass. They don't want even
the smallest thing to give gravity another opportunity to work
against them while they're pushing towards the finish line of a
26.2-mile run.

They are, after all, in it to win it.

The Christian life is a long-distance race that requires perspective, pacing, restraint, and stamina. But to run the race well
and finish the course with speed and agility, something more
is required of serious runners like you and me: a willingness to
"lay aside every encumbrance and the sin which so easily entan-
gles us" (Heb. 12:1) This is one of its key secrets to a life that
is well lived, a race that is well run: a willingness to determine
and discard any interferences that are weighing you down in the
journey.

Check your status to see if you detect any bulkiness that is making you sluggish, perhaps even forcing you to the sidelines far too often to recover from continued exhaustion. Pinpoint any added layers of sins you haven't been willing to jettison—or just those needless encumbrances that are not worth the cost they require for carrying them. Some of these things, you'll find, are even *good* things—your accumulations and habits, preferences and priorities, little likes and luxuries. Determine whether or not they're hindering your freedom of spiritual movement. Too many commitments, too many wastes of time, too many nostalgic bits and pieces, jumbled up with all those little things you do for no other reason than because you've always done them or because other people expect them of you—combined, these can sap your energy, slow your pace, impose unnecessary stress, and cause you to care more about your comfort than your straight-ahead pursuit of the finish line.

> "All things are lawful for me," Paul the apostle said, "but not all things are profitable."

"All things are lawful for me," Paul the apostle said, "but not all things are profitable" (1 Cor. 6:12). The list of possible accessories you could take with you into the coming day have the potential to overload your time capacity and squeeze out any margin needed to make adjustments, take advantage of opportunities, and shift lanes down the road. Be willing to shed some things that will only succeed at holding you back. Because if something is keeping you from being quick on your spiritual feet, is it really worth wearing anymore?

The finish line is up ahead.

Lighten your load and keep your eyes on the prize.

Get rid of the foreign gods that are among you.
Purify yourselves and change your clothes.
GENESIS 35:2 CSB

— He Speaks to Me —

How have you sensed God nudging you to give up something for the sake of your spiritual progress? Even if it's something you really enjoy and can easily justify, ask the Lord to give you His courage and boldness to walk in obedience.

My iniquities are gone over my head;
as a heavy burden they weigh too much for me.
PSALM 38:4

The night is almost gone, and the day is near. Therefore let us lay aside the deeds of darkness and put on the armor of light.
Romans 13:12

Realigning Expectations

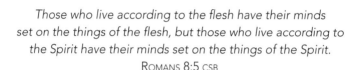

*Those who live according to the flesh have their minds
set on the things of the flesh, but those who live according to
the Spirit have their minds set on the things of the Spirit.*
ROMANS 8:5 CSB

Palm Sunday was the first day in a week of events that would change the whole trajectory of human history. Jesus descended from the Mount of Olives, riding a young colt toward Jerusalem, being celebrated by throngs of people who were gathered to welcome Him as a hero into their city limits.

The Jews had longed for salvation from the oppression they'd faced for centuries: the Assyrians, the Babylonians, the Persians, the Greeks, now the Romans. The tribes of Israel had gone countless generations since they'd known a day when they weren't under the thumb of an imperial juggernaut. And though many Jews were unsure of what this Jesus represented when He emerged on the scene of history, they believed that His objectives were the same as theirs. If establishing His kingdom meant deliverance from Roman rule, they were ready and willing to accept and celebrate His arrival. As long as He was a means to what they wanted, they could overlook a lot of other things they might not understand about Him. The restoration of Israel to her former status of political glory was their aspiration, and they assumed it must be His too.

And so they celebrated His arrival in Jerusalem at that Passover season, conceiving great expectations for His possible rule and reign. Some laid down their coats on the road before Him, while others cut palm branches and placed them at His feet. And all along the way, they were shouting, "Hosanna to the

Son of David; Blessed is He who comes in the name of the LORD; Hosanna in the highest!" (Matt. 21:9).

But days later, they quickly discovered He hadn't come to soften political relations but to soften spiritual hearts. He hadn't come to contend with Roman officials but with religious hypocrites. He hadn't come to reinstate an earthly kingdom but to install a heavenly one, to rescue hurting sinners from eternal death. This same crowd who had honored His entry into Jerusalem would shout "Crucify Him!" as they realized He wouldn't meet their expectations because His agenda was different from theirs.

And usually it still is.

A disparity often exists between our Savior's intentions and our expectations, and a close examination nearly always reveals the reason. We've set our expectations according to a set of flesh-based parameters crafted primarily on the basis of our own interests and desires, expecting His priorities to naturally fall into line. And when they don't, we can sometimes still find ourselves in the angry crowd, more eager to accuse Him than acclaim Him.

> His agenda was different from theirs. And usually it still is.

Palm Sunday reminds us of the ease with which we celebrate Jesus, not because He is truth, but because of our erroneous expectation that He will acquiesce to ours. What's needed of us is a reinvestigation and internal realignment so that our expectations match His promises and priorities. Because when they do, we find our place at the base of His cross, our fleshly desires surrendered, receiving all the deliverance from oppression we could ever want or need.

Let God be found true, though every man be found a liar.
ROMANS 3:4

— He Speaks to Me —

In what areas are you trying to hold Jesus to commitments He never made? Where do the discrepancies exist between your expectations and His promised priorities?

Jesus cried out in the temple, teaching and saying,
"You both know Me and know where I am from; and I
have not come of Myself, but He who sent Me is true."
JOHN 7:28

Flee from youthful lusts and pursue righteousness, faith, love and peace, with those who call on the Lord from a pure heart.
2 TIMOTHY 2:22

Pray for Your Pastor

✤

Brethren, pray for us that the word of the Lord will spread
rapidly and be glorified, just as it did also with you.
2 THESSALONIANS 3:1

Those whom the Lord has given us as pastors—shepherds who disciple us, encourage us, comfort us, and (yes) occasionally need to correct us—have a big job on their hands. No church is perfect, including the ones where you and I regularly worship and stay connected. With people like ourselves, our friends, and our families crowding the pews every week, none of the things about the church that we could find to be critical of can equal the number of things that others could find to be critical of us—the church members. Therefore, most of us know little of the burden our pastors carry each week in fulfilling their role and balancing their lives amid responsibilities and challenges charged to their oversight and care.

Because of this, it's not entirely surprising to hear Paul, in nearly all his letters, imploring the churches he'd established to pray for him "that the message may be given to me when I open my mouth to make known with boldness the mystery of the gospel" (Eph. 6:19 CSB).

And if someone like the apostle Paul was aware of his dependence on prayer, how much more the man who stands in your pulpit.

Too often, many people's inclination is to find fault with their pastor, to question his decisions, to feel slighted by what they feel to be his lack of personal attention. But what a mighty change could occur in all of our hearts—and in the hearts of our pastors as well—if the people of the church were seriously engaged in lifting them before the Lord, asking God to fill their broken, needy places with joyful power and tender sensitivity. Imagine the kind of unity and openness and the unhindered spirit of worship and service that could be unleashed within a church that is consistently prayerful and supportive of its leadership. How beautiful is the congregation who commits to pray for its pastor.

So on this day—when your heart is likely turned toward the many issues in your own home and family and work where many personal needs abound, take a moment to deliberately pray for your pastor and the leadership team at your church. Thank the Lord for placing them here and providing for their work and families. Ask Him to encourage your pastor's heart today, shield him from temptation, inflame him with love for God and His Word, and equip him to love your church dearly and to challenge you well.

How beautiful is the congregation who prays for its pastor.

Thank your Father for not leaving you alone in this daily battle, but for giving you leaders to shepherd you and draw you to Christ.

These courageous souls who have answered the calling of God to lead us, serve us, and walk beside us have offered their shoulders to a broad task. They are helping conform us to the image of Christ. We should help commit them to the keeping and empowering of His Spirit.

I urge that petitions, prayers, intercessions, and thanksgivings be made for everyone, for kings and all those who are in authority.
1 TIMOTHY 2:1 CSB

— He Speaks to Me —

Have you ever asked your church leaders how you could pray for them? The next time you have opportunity, use this space to record what they say and to help you stay faithful in your praying for them.

My house will be called a house of prayer for all the peoples.
Isaiah 56:7

Obey your leaders and submit to them, for they keep watch over your souls as those who will give an account. Let them do this with joy and not with grief, for this would be unprofitable for you.
HEBREWS 13:17

Upriver Realities

The waters which were flowing down from above stood and
rose up in one heap, a great distance away at Adam.
JOSHUA 3:16

When Joshua gave the word for the children of Israel to prepare for a Jordan River crossing, their long national nightmare appeared to be finally over. After decades of roundabout wandering by this generation's forefathers, a new breed of travelers were about to walk a miraculous straight line into the Promised Land.

The people woke up on that expectant morning, brought their entire families with them, and approached the swirling current of the Jordan. The priests who carried the ark of God stepped off the bank into the shallow east edge of the water.

At first it would have appeared as if nothing was happening. The water didn't immediately divide right in front of them, like at the Red Sea crossing. But what the children of Israel didn't know as they craned their necks to the north was that far upstream, God was already working His miracle on their behalf. Though the full force of the Jordan continued to parade by them, clearly hindering a mass river crossing, "the waters which were flowing down from above" had already met the divine dam of God's hand, rising up in a heap roughly thirty miles away. At that distant point, far out of sight, the Jordan was even then starting to become a dry riverbed, while the water that remained ahead continued to drain downstream.

God was moving. God was doing something—though nothing in their physical field of vision could yet testify to it.

From your current vantage point, you may not be able to see how God is working out His purposes in your life. You've gotten your feet wet. You've tried to believe. But life just seems to roll on like always before, oblivious to your prayers and to the faith you've placed in God's ability to change things. But be convinced that even though God may be working "a great distance away," He is working. He hasn't forgotten about you or His promises to you. He has not run into a snag that may prevent Him from following through. The answering may be far away from your sight and impossible as of yet to detect, but be assured that the mighty hand of God's power is already at work on your behalf.

> Even though God may be working "a great distance away," He is working.

Imagine the joy, then, that began to sweep through Israel as someone on the northernmost part of the formation caught sight of the stunning developments in the river. Squeals of delight and excitement would have rippled through the ranks, as the promised word they'd been told but hadn't yet seen was suddenly becoming visible reality.

In time, you will see it with your own eyes, just as the Hebrews did when the remaining waves, stripped of their energy source, emptied out before them like water down a storm drain. And you'll know never again to believe what your eyes alone tell you. You'll always remember that God does things at a distance while you're waiting by faith in your present.

Though you have not seen him, you love him;
though not seeing him now, you believe in him,
and you rejoice with inexpressible and glorious joy.
1 PETER 1:8 CSB

— He Speaks to Me —

What are you waiting on God for right now? What does faith and confidence look like, knowing He's undoubtedly working for you in the distance?

_The vision is yet for the appointed time;
it hastens toward the goal and it will not fail. Though it tarries,
wait for it; for it will certainly come, it will not delay._
HABAKKUK 2:3

I wait for the LORD, my soul does wait, and in His word do I hope.
PSALM 130:5

Start at the Beginning

The fear of the LORD is the beginning of wisdom,
and the knowledge of the Holy One is understanding.
PROVERBS 9:10

More than a dozen times, Proverbs accentuates the imperative value and benefits of fearing the Lord. Over and over again its writer expresses the inestimable significance of esteeming and prioritizing God in all areas of life.

While some earthly authority figures may misuse their power, taking advantage of and even abusing those underneath their care, God always wields His authority in a manner that is congruent with His character of goodness, faithfulness, truth, and love. The expression of this beautiful balance invites us to honor Him without anxiety, worry, or fearful concern that He will ever manipulate us or seek to do us harm. We can relax into an eternal friendship with Him because He is love. He is good. He is faithful. He is true.

But He is indeed GOD—a reality we sometimes overlook because of our pride and to our peril. For while His immanence (nearness) invites us into relationship with Him—and we love Him for that—it comes with the risk of numbing and blinding us to the respect we owe Him and that He should always garner from us. He was and is and will always be transcendent—holy and mighty, beyond humanity, eternally worthy of our allegiance. Remembering this critical fact keeps us resistant to the hubris that robs us of benefits which only come from being in right relationship to Him.

To fear Him combines reverence for His majesty with respect for His power. It involves a grateful honor and esteem that produces quick obedience and submission in us, along with the peace, ease, and freedom of knowing we are well cared for, truly in the best of hands.

And it does something more: it gives us access to the spiritual insights He desires to give us, reserved for those who put Him in a position of priority in their lives.

This is what it means to fear the Lord.

And it is the starting place for the knowledge you seek in understanding His purposes and your life in conjunction with them. When you align yourself with the truth of who He is, He responds to your healthy fear of Him by blessing you not only with "knowledge" and spiritual insight but with the "wisdom" required to use it correctly.

> To fear Him combines reverence for His majesty with respect for His power.

If you want to be led by His Spirit, to be guided into His will, and to walk in the direction of His plans for your life—not some other itinerary you've made up in your head that is taking you off course—then start here with the fear of the Lord. If you don't want to be reckless, careless, or foolish in heart, fear God. If you want to know what He has said, to discern what He is saying, and be able to put it all into wise, consistent practice, fear God.

Being wrapped up in ourselves is the beginning of confusion, failure, and dead ends. But a willingness to reposition Him in a place of honor will realign every other thing in your life.

So start here. And everything else will fall into place.

Everything.

The fear of the LORD is clean, enduring forever; the judgments of the LORD are true; they are righteous altogether.
PSALM 19:9

— He Speaks to Me —

Is there any area of your life where you have not prioritized God and His truth in your life? How can you align your choices, perspectives, and behaviors to honor Him today?

Fear the LORD and serve Him in truth with all your heart;
for consider what great things He has done for you.
1 SAMUEL 12:24

The Spirit of the Lᴏʀᴅ will rest on Him, the spirit of
wisdom and understanding, the spirit of counsel and strength,
the spirit of knowledge and the fear of the Lᴏʀᴅ.
Iᴀᴀɪᴀʜ 11:2

In the Waiting

*You shall not go outside the doorway of the tent of meeting
for seven days, until the day that the period of your ordination
is fulfilled; for he will ordain you through seven days.*
LEVITICUS 8:33

Once we sense God's Spirit leading us in a certain new direction—an exciting kind of work, ministry, focus, or emphasis—we are usually overly eager to get going. The action and opportunities that have been drawing us toward this intriguing phase of life are too tantalizing for us to let unfold organically and slowly. We tend to feel a trickle of anxiety that we are somehow behind in reaching our goal and need to make up for lost time. We become hungry to put our ideas into tangible shape, the way we've dreamed about it ever since the possibility was put up on the drawing board of our minds. We know what He has laid on our hearts to do, and so we want to see it done *now*. Without delay.

And yet any upcoming role or assignment that the Father has assigned to us is primarily His way of initiating a new work *within* us. So while we may be itching to move ahead—ready from the moment the ink is dry or the confirmation is official—we must resist the urge to circumvent the process that is needed to prepare us for the work He is preparing to do through us.

Which means waiting. Trusting.

While He takes action in us.

The priests being ordained in Leviticus 8 were required to stay inside the tent of meeting for seven days, awaiting the completion of what God was doing in their hearts. The purpose of this rite was to consecrate them for their sacred duties—to prepare them inwardly for the service they'd been called to perform outwardly. Those who rushed their preparation, wanting only the position, would not be able to successfully carry out His plans for their lives and their calling long-term. Waiting was—and is—essential to fruitfulness and usefulness.

So even when God is drawing you in a clear direction, don't force your way onto a platform for which you are not yet ready. The best place you can be while waiting for His perfect timing is on the sidelines, taking time to digest what He's teaching you, internalizing the lessons He's been giving you, maturing into the person of integrity He is calling you to become. Yes, the days, weeks, or months of dangling your legs over the edge of God's assignment, listening for the cue to dive in, will test your patience. But waiting until His timing is right ensures that what God is doing in you is given time to work all the way through.

Any role or assignment the Father has assigned to us is primarily His way of initiating a new work within us.

If we hope for what we do not see,
with perseverance we wait eagerly for it.
ROMANS 8:25

— He Speaks to Me —

Where do you sense God leading you now? How can you submit to the preparation process and engage fully in the work He is doing in you?

They all wait for You to give them their food
in due season. You give to them, they gather it up;
You open Your hand, they are satisfied with good.
PSALM 104:27–28

He commanded them not to leave Jerusalem,
but to wait for what the Father had promised.
ACTS 1:4

Challenge Accepted

––––––––––––––– ⚜ –––––––––––––––

*The word of the Lord came to me saying, "Before I formed you
in the womb I knew you, and before you were born I conse-
crated you; I have appointed you a prophet to the nations."*
JEREMIAH 1:4–5

God wants you to experience Him, not just know Him, by allowing you to see His supernatural activity. He wants to show you what it looks and feels like to see Him filling in the gaping margins that are left behind when your abilities run out.

He wants to *challenge* you . . . to show you what He can do when you can't.

Jeremiah is a case in point. He was only a young man when God called him to be His spokesman, and he knew the job was too much for him. He was scared to death to accept God's challenging assignment. But the Lord answered him, "Do not say, 'I am a youth,' because everywhere I send you, you shall go, and all that I command you, you shall speak. Do not be afraid of them"—those people who were sure to find his prophetic words either repulsive or laughable—"for I am with you to deliver you" (vv. 7–8). He did not encourage Jeremiah to concede to his insecurity and weakness, but rather to be assured that divine power would join him in it and take up any slack.

Jeremiah did what many modern saints do not: he believed God and accepted the challenge. He stepped out in obedience. He proclaimed the words that God put in his mouth despite his youth. He told the people of Judah exactly what would happen to them if they did not repent of their sins and turn back to God: the Babylonians would come and destroy Jerusalem and carry them all away into captivity.

323

To be clear, Jeremiah was met with difficulty despite his obedience. In fact, much of the hardship he faced was *because* of it. He suffered more adversity than he thought he was capable of enduring. Yet God gave to him—a naturally timid man—the courage to persevere in the face of severe persecution. He gave him a prophetic word to declare for more than forty years and also divine favor to accomplish the task. Yahweh did then for Jeremiah what He continues to do now for us: extraordinary things through the ordinary lives of anyone willing to step up to the challenge of His will.

This is always what God-sized assignments do—they put us in position to see His miraculous work operating in our frailty. They create opportunities for the power of the Almighty to be manifested through us. And they do something more—they give us the joy and remarkable privilege of seeing Him leap off the pages of Scripture and manifest Himself in the regular experiences of our daily life.

> He wants to challenge you, to show you what He can do when you can't.

God hasn't changed His strategy after all these years. He has always wanted to supernaturally equip His people for challenging tasks. So when these circumstances arise—the kind that will stretch you and require more of you than you think it's possible to give—consider that it might be God speaking to you before you dismiss it. Consider that it might be an invitation giving you the opportunity to see Him in living color in your life. Check inward to see if the Holy Spirit is encouraging you to pursue it despite the challenge it presents.

Because if it is, you are better off on this challenging road *with* His power and favor alongside you than the easier, more convenient route *without* it.

The peace of God, which surpasses all comprehension,
will guard your hearts and your minds in Christ Jesus.
PHILIPPIANS 4:7

— He Speaks to Me —

What are your most common responses to a challenge from God? Self-protection? Fear? Resistance? Delay? What if you simply accepted it as an opportunity to truly experience Him?

Do not worry beforehand about what you are to say,
but say whatever is given you in that hour;
for it is not you who speak, but it is the Holy Spirit.
MARK 13:11

The king spoke and said to Daniel, "Your God whom
you constantly serve will Himself deliver you."
DANIEL 6:16

Quiet on the Home Front

*The boy Samuel served the LORD in Eli's presence. In those
days the word of the LORD was rare and prophetic visions
were not widespread. . . . Then the LORD called Samuel . . .*
1 SAMUEL 3:1, 4 CSB

It still bothers me that God didn't speak to Eli.

If anyone should have been hearing from God in these
long-ago days of Israel's history, it was their high priest at the
holy place of Shiloh. As a Levite, Eli came from a respected lin-
eage. He had presided over Israel's worship for many years. They
looked to him as the mediator between themselves and God,
depending on him for spiritual, economic, even civil instruction.
No one was in a better, more logical place to hear God's voice
and lead the people to follow Him.

But despite Eli's pedigree, his title, and the respect of his
constituents, he was tolerating the evil practices of his two sons,
Hophni and Phineas. Instead of taking his position as priest over
the people and as father of these young men seriously enough to
rein in their abuses toward those who brought their offerings for
sacrifice, he ignored their lack of integrity (1 Sam. 3:13). And
because of this, he received Yahweh's judgment.

Eli's story reminds us that no outward position or acclaim—
not our age, not our reputation, not even our large grasp of Bible
knowledge—is an excuse for tolerating sin. The only thing that
keeps our hearts tender to the workings of God and our ears
open to the whispers of His holiness is purity, humility, honesty,
and receptivity.

Paul explains what happens to people who have a head
knowledge of God but refuse to honor Him with their lives

through obedience. "Even though they knew God, they did not honor Him as God or give thanks, but they became futile in their speculations, and their foolish heart was darkened. Professing to be wise, they became fools" (Rom. 1:21–22).

Thinking themselves wise.

And yet, fools.

Samuel, though only a boy, was different. He was totally committed to doing what was right, and it was evident in the way he lived. He shone like a bright light against the background of the darkness around him—even the spiritual darkness that had descended on the house of the high priest. While Eli was using a light hand on his own sin and the sins in his family, Samuel was living with determined reverence and righteous submission toward the Lord. While others were busy sinning, he was busy obeying God. And to him, God spoke.

> While others were busy sinning, he was busy obeying God.

God isn't looking for perfect people. But He is looking for those who are serious about hearing His Word and obeying it—to those who can truthfully say . . .

Speak, Lord.

I am Your servant.

I am listening.

We are His workmanship, created in Christ Jesus for good works, which God prepared beforehand so that we would walk in them.
EPHESIANS 2:10

— He Speaks to Me —

Is the Spirit bringing to mind an area where you've been resisting Him? Don't ignore it. Acknowledge it. Confess it. Listen and respond.

_____

_____

_____

_____

_____

_____

_____

_____

_____

_____

_____

*Your sins have hidden His face from
you so that He does not hear.*
Isaiah 59:2

A cloud formed, overshadowing them, and a voice came out of the cloud, "This is My beloved Son, listen to Him!"
MARK 9:7

Language Lessons

✿
---

*"The good man out of the good treasure of his
heart brings forth what is good; and the evil man out
of the evil treasure brings forth what is evil; for his
mouth speaks from that which fills his heart."*
LUKE 6:45

Jesus' use of the word *heart* signifies the inner being of an individual, the place where our thoughts, attitudes, and beliefs are cemented. The heart is a reservoir, a holding tank for every thought we've ever placed there, particularly those we've allowed to solidify and make their home there. It's a storehouse containing the essence of who we are and—because of the heart's direct link to our ongoing habits and actions—it is the picture of who we are becoming.

If we're ever not sure who that someone is, all we need to do is listen to ourselves . . . because our words and tones of voice and topics of conversation will tell us what is hidden within. Just as floodwaters burst through a dam, just as sizzling popcorn kernels erupt on the cooktop, the contents of our hearts will inevitably push and press, unable to stay contained, eventually spilling out in the things we say. For the "mouth speaks from that which fills the heart."

So we must be mindful of what we allow inside.

This "treasure"—whether "good" or "evil"—is truly a crucial component of life.

The word in the original language is the same term used to describe the "treasures" that the wise men presented to Jesus (Matt. 2:11). Obviously the reason those treasures were able to be taken out as gifts to the Messiah was because the Magi had carefully chosen and packed them inside before they left. The gold and myrrh and frankincense had ridden with them the entire way—preserved so that they could be presented to Jesus. Likewise, the conversation, reactions, and expressions we offer our Savior will be congruent with whatever we have harbored inside. If we want them to be equally beautiful and precious in the Lord's sight as the Magi's gifts, we must be careful to watch what we're carrying.

Therefore, guard your heart, and do not allow it to become hardened (Prov. 28:14), deceptive (Ps. 12:2), prideful (Prov. 21:4), or unclean (Ps. 51:10). Seek rather to nurture a heart that's sensitive to the prodding of God's Spirit (Rom. 8:5), single-mindedly devoted to Him (Ps. 86:11), drenched in humility (Prov. 22:4), and pure all the way down to the motive (Matt. 5:8). "Do nothing from selfishness or empty conceit, but with humility of mind regard one another as more important than yourselves; do not merely look out for your own personal interests, but also for the interests of others" (Phil. 2:3–4).

> Don't just watch your mouth; watch your heart.

When our hearts are full of gratitude and humility, certain of God's love, and when we genuinely prize the worth of those around us, we will release a steady stream of graciousness that refreshes others through everything we say. It will come from what's rooted in our treasure box, which we've been sure to keep filled with a wealth of good things.

So don't just watch your mouth; watch your heart. And the right words will always be found on your lips.

Watch over your heart with all diligence,
for from it flow the springs of life.
PROVERBS 4:23

— He Speaks to Me —

What have you been most consistently putting inside your heart lately? How have you seen the direct result of that? What proactive measures can you put in place to be mindful about storing good treasures in your heart?

Sanctify Christ as Lord in your hearts, always being ready to make a defense to everyone who asks you to give an account for the hope that is in you, yet with gentleness and reverence.
1 Peter 3:15

*Let your speech always be with grace,
as though seasoned with salt, so that you
will know how you should respond to each person.*
COLOSSIANS 4:6

In the Now

———————— ⚜ ————————

But You are the same, and Your years
will not come to an end.
HEBREWS 1:12

God is eternally in the *now*.

Everything exists before Him in a perpetual present tense.

Therefore, unlike us, nothing catches Him off guard. He is never delayed or behind schedule. So if you're currently feeling rushed or hurried about a decision that needs your input, and your next step is not rooted in a deep confidence of inner peace, this alone could be an indication that God has probably not spoken yet. And though other people or circumstances may be exerting pressure on you to move quickly or declare your intentions, bravely hang on to your belief that God has no need to guide you in a hasty manner, and that He will speak to you at the appropriate time. With clarity and conviction.

The voice of the enemy will coerce and force, using the tactics of fear and intimidation. He will always accentuate the mistakes of the past and plant fear about the what-ifs of the future. The voice of God, on the other hand, gently guides and woos, pointing to the blessings and opportunities He is inviting you into today.

Much of our frustration in hearing God centers around the issue of *timing*. We want to know more than He wants to reveal. And we want to know it *now*. Yet He speaks to us progressively, on a need-to-know basis, giving us just enough light for the next step. So we must trust Him until He sovereignly determines to unfold another layer of His will and direction to us. And when the time is right for us to know more, we'll know it. Until then, the things that are "freely given to us by God" (1 Cor. 2:12) are the only things we need for victory. These are the things we need to know *now* and to which we will be held accountable *now*.

Breathe deeply with the knowledge that His purposes have been specifically calculated with both you and His larger designs in mind. Then allow yourself the freedom to sit back and wait with a holy confidence, assured that this is the pace of His will for your life today.

Many Christians—even the most active, diligent ones—while well-intentioned in their pursuit to hear God, are living tense, fearful lives. They are worried that they're missing "God's will for my life." They nervously look high and low for spiritual specifics, then grow dismayed when they can't find the answers in their own timing. Even with a clear conscience to guide them, they're sure they are somehow secretly, subtly failing God, or else He'd be more forthcoming, telling them everything they want to know right now. But if you don't know more yet, it's likely because you don't need to know yet. Be committed to the last thing you heard Him say! This is His will.

> He speaks progressively, giving us just enough light for the next step.

And if you aren't clear on something, stay put. Don't move. Give yourself permission to wait, remembering that waiting is not the same as inactivity. Waiting is a commitment to continue on in obedience until God speaks. Only when God has spoken to you will you be cued to change direction. Until then, as the old hymn goes . . . Trust and obey / For there's no other way / To be happy in Jesus / Than to trust and obey.

Your word is a lamp to my feet and a light to my path.
PSALM 119:105

— He Speaks to Me —

What's a current (or coming) decision that's causing you to feel time pressure to answer it? What are the elements of God's guidance that you already know, and how are you responding obediently to those?

In a very little while, He who is coming will come, and will not delay. But My righteous one shall live by faith.
HEBREWS 10:37–38

There is an appointed time for everything.
And there is a time for every event under heaven.
ECCLESIASTES 3:1

Even That Thing

---❦---

Be anxious for nothing, but in everything by prayer and supplica-
tion with thanksgiving let your requests be made known to God.
PHILIPPIANS 4:6

God's activity is not confined to the spectacular and
jaw-dropping. He does a plethora of things that never make
headlines or invite peals of applause. Some of His work—dare I
say, some of His *best* work—is performed on the most ordinary
days, in the most ordinary places and ways, with ordinary people. Like us.

The tendency of humanity is to put God into our self-established
theological box into which we hope He will comfortably fit, a box
that doesn't allow for the supernatural and amazing . . . because *that*
is too big. But sometimes the box we've chosen doesn't make room
for Him to work in the routine and ordinary. *That* is too small.

Yet a God-box is still a God-box, no matter where you position it in your faith. Limiting our view of Him to the stupendous
is not really any different from limiting our view of Him to the
monotonous. He doesn't exist only in the stratosphere of extravagant need. His ability comes all the way down to the ground, to
the places we live on regular weekdays while working, playing,
eating, and engaging in ordinary realities.

By no means does this understanding minimize Him to a
trivial fraction of who He is. It actually magnifies the detailed
and caring nature of His character. The same God who divided
the Red Sea is the same God who knows about the loss of a solitary, fallen sparrow and takes the time to number the hairs on
our heads (Matt. 10:29–30). He knows when His children are
in grave agony, just as He knows and cares when it has simply

been one of those really long mornings. Nothing escapes His attention. Nothing is too small to avoid His notice. He cares about it all.

In highlighting His attention to routine detail, the Scripture counteracts a lie we find so easy to believe—that God may have been loving enough to send His Son to die for us, taking care of our *biggest* thing, but He's not much interested in taking care of our little things, our daily things, our too-small-to-mention things. Yet "He who did not spare His own Son, but delivered Him over for us all, how will He not also with Him freely give us all things?" (Rom. 8:32).

> A God-box is still a God-box, no matter where you position it.

There's a comprehensiveness to God's ability that covers all that concerns us. "He forgives all your iniquity; he heals all your diseases" (Ps. 103:3 csb). He invites "all who are weary and heavy-laden" to come experience His rest (Matt. 11:28). He says His lovingkindness "will follow me all the days of my life" (Ps. 23:6), and that if we seek His kingdom above every other desire, "all these things" will be given (Matt. 6:33)—full provision, food and clothing, love and shelter, every need.

He who is saving you from hell is also willing and able to save what's left of your nerves and your workweek. Because even in the fine print of Scripture, we can trace the detailed care and concern of our God for everything we face.

Even that thing.

The mundane thing.

The ordinary thing.

The small thing.

> *The Lord will accomplish what concerns me;*
> *Your lovingkindness, O Lord, is everlasting.*
> Psalm 138:8

— He Speaks to Me —

What are some things you don't often vocalize to God in prayer because you think they're too insignificant to bring up? Trust Him specifically with even those things today.

In everything give thanks; for this is
God's will for you in Christ Jesus.
1 Thessalonians 5:18

He counts the number of the stars;
He gives names to all of them.
Psalm 147:4

Desperate Encounters

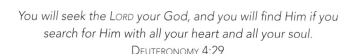

You will seek the LORD your God, and you will find Him if you
search for Him with all your heart and all your soul.
DEUTERONOMY 4:29

Word circulated that Jesus would be passing through Jericho one day, and a diminutive tax collector named Zacchaeus wanted to catch a glimpse of Him. Desperate, the man climbed a tree so he wouldn't miss what his heart was hoping to behold. Jesus saw him there, perched in the tree, and called to him as He passed by: "Zacchaeus, hurry and come down, for today I must stay at your house" (Luke 19:5).

Bartimaeus, an outcast and blind man, was also passionate about "seeing" Jesus. Sitting at his usual begging post, he heard the commotion of people excitedly streaming into town hoping to get a look at the stranger who was said to be the Messiah. When Bartimaeus heard that it was Jesus passing by, he cried out, "Jesus, Son of David, have mercy on me!" (Luke 18:38)—loud enough that he embarrassed the other townspeople, who wanted to give Jesus a dignified welcome. But his persistence caught the ear of the traveling Savior, and a blind beggar received his sight.

In the Old Testament, when God tested the Israelite travelers, threatening to abandon them in the desert after their worship of a golden calf, it was the desperation of Moses pleading with Him—"If Your presence does not go with us, do not lead us up from here" (Exod. 33:15)—that galvanized God's continued presence among the people. Moses didn't want the Promised Land without the Promise Giver. And in response to His servant's desperation, God said, "I will do this very thing you have asked, for you have found favor with me, and I know you by name" (v. 17 csb). He dazzled Moses with His glory in the cleft of the rock—with more of His visible presence than anyone had ever seen.

Perhaps what we lack more than anything else these days is what these three people had.

Holy desperation.

Clearly, God responds to it. He wants our relationship with Him to be our consuming passion—what we think about, what we talk about, what we're constantly hungry for more of and willing to do anything for—because He knows once we've experienced His manifest presence, our appetites will be whetted for more. And more.

> He wants our relationship with Him to be our consuming passion.

Those in the Scripture who didn't let obstacles become excuses for not seeking Him, or back down at others' disapproval of their unabashed appeals for mercy, or give in to the despair of delay but latched on to Him for dear life—they received what God was obviously willing to give them. Wonder what He is ready to give *you* if only you will seek Him more desperately? More passionately? More fully?

> Call to Me and I will answer you, and I will tell you
> great and mighty things, which you do not know.
> JEREMIAH 33:3

— He Speaks to Me —

What would the people who know you describe as your consuming passion?

I count all things to be loss in view of the surpassing
value of knowing Christ Jesus my Lord.
PHILIPPIANS 3:8

Blessed are you who hunger now, for you shall be satisfied.
Blessed are you who weep now, for you shall laugh.
LUKE 6:21

Let It Rain

He will come to us like the rain,
like the spring rain watering the earth.
HOSEA 6:3

The clouds were already dense and dark when I left the house that morning. Undaunted, I tried to squeeze in my morning run before the nasty weather hit. And as I watched those pregnant clouds looming low on the horizon ready to burst at any moment with a cleansing shower—drenching, refreshing, renewing the earth—I found myself prompted to prayer. Beckoned by God's Spirit, I asked for His presence to hang low in my life like those clouds, to burst open so that the floodgate of heaven could dispense every blessing and promise He intends to give. Between breaths, I asked God to allow His glory to rain on me just as the rain was soon to fall on our neighborhood.

Then suddenly, the immediate gush of a full downpour.

There were no tentative sprinkles preparing for the thunderstorm. Just, all at once, the heavens opened. Instinctively I tore for home, covering my head as best I could while dashing for the warmth of shelter.

Yet even as I ran, the Spirit spoke to me again, shocking me with the poignancy of the thought. *This is what My people do,* He seemed to be saying. *They pray for rain, and when it pours, they run back to the place they came from.*

How true that is. We want God to move. We beg Him to. We pray with boldness that the cloak of complacency will be removed from our hearts, that the windows of heaven will open. We pray for Him to display His glory and power to us and through us. We anxiously await His wonders in our everyday living, not wanting to settle for dutiful religion. But if His showing up comes unexpectedly, causing us a bit of discomfort, drawing us out of the familiar ruts where we pace ourselves to the safe, steady rhythm of our spiritual disciplines, we become unsettled and out of sorts. We duck for cover instead of abandoning ourselves to the outpouring of His Spirit that He has sovereignly chosen to release. This kind of display was not exactly what we meant when we asked for more of Him. We wanted to be in more control of the timing, able to regulate the amount of impact, turning it off when we thought we'd had enough.

My heart was racing with conviction as I ran. So, still short of my house, I slowed to a stop on the sidewalk even though the rain continued its noisy hammering. I stood beneath the pouring heavens, I opened my arms wide, and I turned my face upward into the falling raindrops. Then with His Word stirring like a roaring fire within me, I began praying a prayer that I'd love you to pray with me right now.

> Forgive me for ever running back to the familiar comforts that take me away from You.

"Lord, let it rain. And when it does, give me the courage to stand under the heavens with my arms outstretched to Your work. Cause me to be willing to go where You take me, even if the path is uncomfortable or unfamiliar. Tear down any man-made obstacles that keep me from seeing You fully. Open my heart to receive anything that draws me closer to You. Let me be drenched by your Spirit . . . and forgive me for ever running back to the familiar comforts that take me away from You."

Send rain, Lord.

We're standing. Waiting. Watching.

Will You not Yourself revive us again,
that Your people may rejoice in You?
PSALM 85:6

— He Speaks to Me —

Don't be afraid to pray for rain. What will you do when it starts
to fall?

_Ground that drinks the rain that often falls on it and
that produces vegetation useful to those for whom
it is cultivated receives a blessing from God._
HEBREWS 6:7 CSB

*Behold, I will do something new, now it will
spring forth; will you not be aware of it? I will even make
a roadway in the wilderness, rivers in the desert.*
Isaiah 43:19

Goodness Knows

---

*The L*ORD *is righteous in all His ways and kind in all His deeds.*
PSALM 145:17

The tumor is still there.

Your family is still in crisis.

The church is still without a pastor.

Your son or daughter still can't find work.

It's one thing to believe that God is able to do anything He wants. He is God. You know that. But it is quite another thing to believe that He is willing and able to do it *for you*.

No matter what we want our relationship with God and His actions toward us to be, it will always come down to a matter of trust—trusting that He is able, and trusting that His kindness toward us makes Him willing in His infinite wisdom to do what is best for us. He can see beyond what we can see, and He can love us without explaining why His love needs to look like *this* at the moment.

Please hear this following statement with the gentleness I intend: Whether or not God *chooses* to do something is a question of His *sovereignty*, not His ability. Whether or not He *will* do it is *His* business. But believing that He *can*—that's *our* business.

You and I—so often walking around with a focus on the severity and heaviness of our problems—have no idea the activity that God is currently orchestrating in our lives, not to mention the protective rescues He has already accomplished. He may have healed you of sicknesses you didn't even know you were carrying. He may have rectified circumstances on your behalf before you were even aware you had a problem. Wonder what

God has already done for you today without even telling you? Just because He loves you?

According to Scripture, this One who is "righteous in all His ways" is also "kind in all His deeds." And while He may allow things into your life that are decidedly not good on the surface, His Word promises He is working all things together *for* your good in Christ (Rom. 8:28). His heart is brimming over with compassion and affection for you. He calls you the "apple" of His eye (Ps. 17:8), and is so endeared to you that He lifts His voice to sing songs over you (Zeph. 3:17). You are His "beloved" (Rom. 9:25), and His "banner" over you is "love" (Song of Sol. 2:4). He is constantly bringing about the finest results in your circumstances, even though His methods may defy human understanding.

> Wonder what God has already done for you today without even telling you?

Just because you can't see it or feel it or explain how this latest development is a sure sign of His kindness toward you means only one thing: not that He is unable, but that His sovereign love is at work right now in some other way. And as you become willing to trust this truth, it will put you in the most receptive position of all for watching Him work . . . for seeing everything He is capable of.

The sons of Israel will return and seek the LORD their God and David their king; and they will come trembling to the LORD and to His goodness in the last days.
HOSEA 3:5

— He Speaks to Me —

How has God shown His kindness in ways that weren't initially visible in times past but became evident later? How can this insight help you in your hard-to-understand moments today?

Gracious is the LORD, and righteous;
yes, our God is compassionate.
PSALM 116:5

*"I will fill the soul of the priests with abundance, and My people
will be satisfied with My goodness,"* declares the LORD.

JEREMIAH 31:14

The Summit and Beyond

———————— ✲ ————————

Now to Him who is able to do far more abundantly beyond
all that we ask or think, according to the power that works
within us, to Him be the glory in the church and in
Christ Jesus to all generations forever and ever. Amen.
EPHESIANS 3:20–21

R eading the book of Ephesians is like climbing a mountain. One chapter, two chapters, three chapters—each
one building on the other, declaring in powerful prose
the indescribable riches freely bestowed by our loving, gracious
Father on all who believe in Christ. Then just when you think
you've read of every major blessing that a holy God could possibly give to undeserving sinners like us, you reach the breathtaking summit in mid-book: the reality of living on this earth
in intimate relationship with Him "who is able to do far more
abundantly beyond all that we ask or think."

Continuing into chapter four, you prepare for your descent
from this doxology, except a word appears that unlocks new
vistas which only those on the pinnacle can see. It promises that
there are higher heights to survey in Him. Such is the abundance
inherent in the word, "Therefore . . ."

The back half of Ephesians is not a descent after all. It is
actually an intense and beautiful description of all the treasures
that came before it. It reveals how, based on what our limitless
God has done to redeem, equip, and draw close to us, we are
now empowered to "walk in a manner worthy of the calling"
that we've received in Christ Jesus (Eph. 4:1). We can now
legitimately be people who are patient and gentle, loving and
accepting, utterly at peace and contented in life (4:2–5). We can

serve others in a way that fulfills God's purposes and produces unity and spiritual fruit in the process (4:11–16). We can stifle our anger, be scrupulously honest, extend true forgiveness, and be the same pure, upright person in private as we claim to be in public (4:25–32). We can renew the love in our marriages, refashioning our relationship into one that honors God in every way (5:22–33). We can parent our children with caring responsibility, perform all our work with diligence and integrity, and treat others with tender understanding from a heart of growing character (6:1–8).

All of these things can be ours when we start putting the power within us to work.

Much of what you may be asking God to change in you today, He has already begun transforming. The key that unlocks these answers and outcomes is in Him. And since He is already in you by His Spirit, no longer do you need to treat symptoms, patch up problem areas, paper things over, and get along the best you know how. You need only to start operating in the power He has granted you as His child, and then you are on your way to witnessing the steady growth of spiritual transformation you've been struggling so hard to generate yourself.

> Much of what you may be asking God to change in you today, He has already begun transforming.

That's what the "therefore" is there for—to show you the Spirit-infused potential you now have through Christ to become the person He created you to be—to prepare you to "be strong in the Lord and in the strength of His might" (6:10).

I can do all things through Him who strengthens me.
PHILIPPIANS 4:13

— He Speaks to Me —

What do you most desire to see change in your character, demeanor, and self-control? How does an Ephesians perspective bring it into reach for you?

For by You I can run upon a troop;
and by my God I can leap over a wall.
PSALM 18:29

*My God will supply all your needs according
to His riches in glory in Christ Jesus.*
PHILIPPIANS 4:19

Blinded by the Light

--- ✤ ---

"Those who were with me saw the light, to be sure, but did not understand the voice of the One who was speaking to me."
ACTS 22:9

The apostle Paul described what is arguably the most amazing conversion story in all of Christian history: "As I was on my way, approaching Damascus about noontime"—heading out on mission to round up Christians and bring them back to Jerusalem as prisoners—"a very bright light suddenly flashed from heaven all around me, and I fell to the ground and heard a voice saying to me, 'Saul, Saul, why are you persecuting me?'" (Acts 22:6–7).

That's how a man feared by the early followers of Jesus because of his brutal hatred for their beliefs became their most prominent evangelist, defender, and writer of half the books in the New Testament. His passions changed, his heart changed, his mission changed, even his name changed. Nothing was ever the same again for Paul after he was blinded by that light from heaven on the road to Damascus.

But not everyone who witnessed those eye-popping moments was impacted the same way. Others who were traveling with him said they saw the light, heard a noise, knew that something strange was happening, but they couldn't make out the sound as actual words. What's more, since the brightness of the light rendered Paul unable to see, he needed to be "led by the hand by those who were with me" (v. 11)—companions of his who obviously still *could* see, despite having seen the same light that Paul did.

What a tragedy to see the light but not be changed by it.

Blinded by it.

An encounter with God is meant to change us. To stagger us. To blind us to old pursuits, interests, ambitions, and fleshly desires, while miraculously opening our internal vision to eternal pursuits. What a waste to simply get up and go back to our normal habits after being in His presence and sensing the exhilaration of His nearness—after powerful moments in His Word, in prayer, in places where He's made His way so plain to us. When His light shines and His voice speaks on *this* road, it should alter our experience, our choices, and our direction on the road ahead.

> What a tragedy to see the light but not be changed by it.

Don't settle for being someone who only sees the light but then keeps walking in the same direction and with the same vision as before. Be *blinded* to whatever has dulled your spiritual passion or led you down side roads that are taking you away from your calling. Look and be transformed. And turn a blind eye to everything else.

*We all, with unveiled face, beholding as in a mirror
the glory of the Lord, are being transformed into the same
image from glory to glory, just as from the Lord, the Spirit.*
2 CORINTHIANS 3:18

— He Speaks to Me —

As you've journeyed through this devotional, what have you been "blinded" to? What have your spiritual eyes been "opened" to?

The unfolding of Your words gives light;
it gives understanding to the simple.
Psalm 119:130

The eye is the lamp of your body; when your eye is clear,
your whole body also is full of light;
but when it is bad, your body also is full of darkness.
Luke 11:34

DISCERNING THE

Voice
of God

HOW TO RECOGNIZE WHEN GOD SPEAKS

PRISCILLA SHIRER

REVISED AND EXPANDED

In this new edition, you'll find all-new:

- Teaching videos
- Weekly articles by Dr. Tony Evans
- In-depth stories and illustrations
- Exercises to equip you post-study

Bible Study Book	005797596	$12.99
Leader Kit	005797597	$149.99

AVAILABLE WHERE STUDIES ARE SOLD.